United Nations Conference on Trade and Development

# Investment Policy Review

# Sierra Leone

**UNITED NATIONS**

New York and Geneva, 2010

# NOTE

UNCTAD serves as the focal point within the United Nations Secretariat for all matters related to foreign direct investment, as part of its work on trade and development. This function was formerly carried out by the United Nations Centre on Transnational Corporations (1975–1992). UNCTAD's work is carried out through intergovernmental deliberations, research and analysis, and technical assistance activities.

The term "country" as used in this study also refers, as appropriate, to territories or areas; the designations employed and the presentation of the material do not imply the expression of any opinion whatsoever on the part of the Secretariat of the United Nations concerning the legal status of any country, territory, city or area or of its authorities, or concerning the delimitation of its frontiers or boundaries. In addition, the designations of country groups are intended solely for statistical or analytical convenience and do not necessarily express a judgment about the stage of development reached by a particular country or area in the development process.

The following symbols have been used in the tables:
Two dots (..) indicate that data are not available or not separately reported. Rows in tables have been omitted in those cases where no data are available for any of the elements in the row.
A hyphen (-) indicates that the item is equal to zero or its value is negligible.
A blank in a table indicates that the item is not applicable.
A slash (/) between dates representing years – for example, 2004/05, indicates a financial year.
Use of a dash (–) between dates representing years – for example, 2004–2005 – signifies the full period involved, including the beginning and end years.
Reference to the "dollars" ($) means United States dollars, unless otherwise indicated.
Annual rates of growth or change, unless otherwise stated, refer to annual compound rates.
Details and percentages in tables do not necessarily add to totals because of rounding.
The material contained in this study may be freely quoted with appropriate acknowledgement.

| UNCTAD/DIAE/PCB/2009/14 |
| --- |

| UNITED NATIONS PUBLICATION |
| --- |
| Sales No. E.10.II.D.8 |
| ISBN 978-92-1-112785-0 |

# PREFACE

The UNCTAD Investment Policy Reviews are intended to help countries improve their investment policies and familiarize governments and the international private sector with an individual country's investment environment. The reviews are considered by the UNCTAD Commission on Investment, Enterprise and Development.

The Investment Policy Review of Sierra Leone, initiated at the request of the government, was carried out through a fact-finding mission in June 2008. The mission received the full cooperation of the relevant ministries and agencies, in particular the Ministry of Trade and Industry and the Sierra Leone Investment and Export Promotion Agency (SLIEPA). The mission also benefitted from the views of the private sector, foreign and domestic, and the resident international community, particularly bilateral donors and development agencies. A preliminary version of this report was discussed with stakeholders at a national workshop in Freetown on 9 October 2009. The final report reflects written comments from various Ministries of the Government of Sierra Leone, as collected by the Ministry of Trade and Industry and SLIEPA.

The suitability and effectiveness of the regulatory regime is assessed against the following criteria: (a) adequate promotion and protection of the public interest; (b) adequate promotion of investment and sustainable socio-economic development; and (c) effectiveness and implementation of methods employed, given the public interest, development objectives and the legitimate concerns of investors that rules and procedures do not unduly burden their competitiveness. International practices are used as benchmark when making the assessment and proposing recommendations in the report.

The review also concentrates on the development of an overall strategy for the attraction and retention of foreign direct investment. This follows a specific request from the Government of Sierra Leone.

This report was prepared by the Investment Policy Review team under the supervision of Chantal Dupasquier. James Zhan provided overall guidance. Mario Berrios, Paige Griffin and Craig Van Grasstek drafted the report, which benefited from substantive contributions from Rory Allan, Alexandre de Crombrugghe, Quentin Dupriez, Anna Joubin-Bret, Massimo Meloni and Violeta Mitova. Farrel Elliott, a local consultant, and Da Huo provided research assistance. Comments and suggestions were received from UNCTAD colleagues, including Joachim Karl and George Lipimile, within the context of an internal peer review process. It was funded by the Governments of Ireland and Sweden, which also provided financing for some follow-up activities.

It is hoped that the analysis and recommendations of this review will help Sierra Leone achieve its development goals, contribute to improved policies, promote dialogue among stakeholders and catalyse investment and the beneficial impact of FDI.

*Geneva, November 2009*

# CONTENTS

## TABLES

## FIGURES

## BOXES

# ABBREVIATIONS

| | |
|---|---|
| ARIPO | African Regional Industrial Property Organization |
| ASYCUDA | Automated system for customs data |
| BIT | Bilateral investment treaty |
| BOT | Build-operate-and-transfer |
| DFID | Department for International Development, United Kingdom |
| DTT | Double taxation treaty |
| ECOWAS | Economic Community of West African States |
| EIA | Environment impact assessment |
| EU | European Union |
| EUCORD | European Cooperative for Rural Development |
| FAO | Food and Agriculture Organization of the United Nations |
| FIAS | Foreign Investment Advisory Service (World Bank) |
| FDI | Foreign direct investment |
| GATS | General Agreement on Trade in Services |
| GDP | Gross domestic product |
| GFCF | Gross fixed capital formation |
| ICSID | International Centre for Settlement of Investment Disputes |
| ILO | International Labour Organization |
| IMF | International Monetary Fund |
| IPA | Investment promotion agency |
| IPR | Investment policy review |
| ITC | International Trade Centre |
| ITU | International Telecommunication Union |
| MAGS | Mining and General Services Limited |
| MDG | Millennium Development Goal |
| NCP | National Commission for Privatization |
| NEPAD | New Partnership for Africa's Development |
| NPA | National Power Authority |
| NRA | National Revenue Authority |
| NGO | Non-governmental organization |
| OECD | Organization for Economic Cooperation and Development |
| PCT | Patent cooperation treaty |
| PPP | Private-public partnership |
| PRSP | Poverty Reduction Strategy Paper |
| PSI | Pre-shipment inspection |
| SLIEPA | Sierra Leone Investment and Export Promotion Agency |
| SLMA | Sierra Leone Maritime Administration |
| SLNSC | Sierra Leone National Shipping Company |
| SLPA | Sierra Leone Port Authority |
| SME | Small and medium-sized enterprises |
| SNA | Sierra Leone Airlines Limited |
| TNC | Transnational corporation |
| TRG | Titanium Resources Group Limited |
| TRIPS | Trade-related intellectual property rights |
| UNDP | United Nations Development Programme |
| UNESCO | United Nations Educational, Scientific and Cultural Organization |
| VAT | Value added tax |
| WTO | World Trade Organization |

# SIERRA LEONE

## Key investment climate indicators (2010)

| Economy | Sierra Leone | Ghana | Guinea | ECO-WAS |
|---|---|---|---|---|
| Starting business time (days) | 12.0 | 33.0 | 41.0 | 40.1 |
| Cost of registering property (% of property value) | 12.4 | 1.1 | 13.9 | 12.3 |
| Investor protection index (0–10) | 6.3 | 6.0 | 2.7 | 3.9 |
| Rigidity of employment index (0–100) | 41.0 | 27.0 | 24.0 | 37.3 |
| Difficulty of hiring index (0–100) | 33.0 | 11.0 | 33.0 | 39.5 |
| Difficulty of redundancy index (0–100) | 50.0 | 50.0 | 20.0 | 40.7 |
| Redundancy costs (weeks of salary) | 189.0 | 178.0 | 26.0 | 66.1 |
| Cost of enforcing contracts (% of claim) | 149.5 | 23.0 | 45.0 | 49.6 |
| Time to export (days) | 26.0 | 19.0 | 33.0 | 27.2 |
| Time to import (days) | 31.0 | 29.0 | 32.0 | 31.5 |
| Domestic investment (% GDP)[1] | 16.0 | 34.9 | 14.7 | 20.5 |

*Sources:* World Bank, Doing Business and UNCTAD. Note: 1 Data for 2007.

## Key economic and social indicators

| Indicator | 1980–1989 average | 1990–1999 average | 2007 | ECOWAS 2007 |
|---|---|---|---|---|
| Population (millions) | 3.6 | 4.0 | 5.4 | 280.9 |
| GDP at market prices (billions of dollars) | 1.3 | 1.1 | 1.9 | 255.8 |
| GDP per capita (dollars) | 364.0 | 279.4 | 357.0 | 910.6 |
| Real GDP growth (%) | 2.8 | -7.3 | 6.5 | 4.7 |
| GDP by sector (%): | | | | |
| Agriculture | 42.5 | 40.9 | 51.0 | 32.6 |
| Industry | 10.6 | 11.0 | 10.6 | 36.8 |
| Services | 46.9 | 48.1 | 38.4 | 30.6 |
| Trade (millions of dollars): | | | | |
| Merchandise exports | 138.7 | 78.5 | 245.2 | 81 252.07 |
| Services exports | 34.3 | 55.7 | 42.1 | 13 229.24 |
| Merchandise imports | 212.8 | 136.7 | 444.7 | 69 226.73 |
| Services imports | 50.5 | 75.8 | 94.2 | 23 884.92 |
| Export of goods and services (% of GDP) | 12.7 | 20.6 | 13.4 | 41.0 |
| Import of goods and services (% of GDP) | 18.3 | 21.6 | 28.3 | 28.5 |
| Capital flows (millions of dollars): | | | | |
| Net FDI flows | -13.2 | 3.4 | 94.5 | 8 306.9 |
| Net flows from private creditors | 2.1 | -2.4 | 0.0 | 285.9 |
| Net flows from official creditors | 20.7 | 37.7 | 18.9 | 1 492.5 |
| Grants, including technical cooperation | 58.9 | 90.2 | 1 077.8 | 8 097.1 |
| FDI inflows (% of GDP) | -1.0 | 0.3 | 4.9 | 6.3 |
| Life expectancy at birth (years) | 38.9 | 39.1 | 47.3 | 55.2 |
| Infant mortality rate (per thousand life births) | 178.2 | 166.9 | 159.2[1] | 100.8[1] |

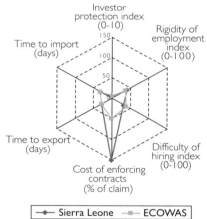

*Sierra Leone* — ECOWAS

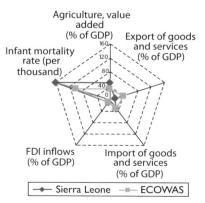

*Sierra Leone* — ECOWAS

*Sources:* UNCTAD; World Bank, Global Development Finance, World Development Indicators. Note: 1 Data for 2006.

# INTRODUCTION

The civil war that ended in 2002 inflicted significant damages to Sierra Leone's investment and growth potential. Its low ranking in the Human Development Index illustrates the severity of Sierra Leone's poverty conditions.

Since the end of the war, the government has committed to re-establishing the conditions that would enable the economic and social development of the country. However, the country's small domestic market, undiversified economic structure, poor infrastructure and unskilled labour force continue to contrast with its rich natural endowments and privileged maritime geographical position. So far, the economy relies essentially on exports of minerals, the only sector that has witnessed a limited foreign direct investment (FDI) presence. In this context, a major challenge for the Government of Sierra Leone is to adopt policies to sustain the high economic growth experienced in the immediate post-war period. In this regard, many initiatives have been undertaken and FDI has been recognized as a key element of the country's growth prospect. Until now however, there has been no overall FDI strategy or concerted efforts in place to facilitate FDI entry.

The global economic slowdown will impact investment flows, making it even more challenging for Sierra Leone to increase FDI inflows in the near term. While this temporary impact is unavoidable, Sierra Leone should continue with its reform agenda. This would enable the country to be better positioned for the period of economic recovery and would also be useful in maintaining current levels of FDI. Even though major legal reforms began in 2000, the limited institutional capacity made it difficult to adequately and effectively sequence and implement the proposed measures. It is against this background that the Government of Sierra Leone requested UNCTAD to undertake an Investment Policy Review (IPR) and to come up with concrete policy recommendations to attract and benefit from FDI.

The structure of the report is as follows. Chapter I presents an overview of the economic structure and the impact of FDI. The domestic economy remains small and dominated by agriculture; the secondary and tertiary sectors are underdeveloped and provide little formal employment. The tremendous deficit in infrastructure constitutes a key constraint that significantly limits the country's capacity to exploit its abundant natural resources. This contributes to high operating costs that, in addition to the small domestic market and the absence of industrial and services sectors, limit the capacity to attract investment from major transnational corporations (TNCs). However, small FDI flows from neighbouring countries, particularly the Economic Community of West African States (ECOWAS), have started in recent years and represent, at least in the short run, a more realistic FDI potential.

Chapter II examines the investment framework. Sierra Leone already has in place a regime open to FDI and an ongoing ambitious reform programme to improve the conditions to attract and benefit from FDI. Although important progress has been made, a number of shortcomings still exist. To address them, this chapter proposes a number of recommendations to deepen the reforms and to position Sierra Leone's investment framework on more competitive grounds.

Chapter III proposes an overall strategy to enhance the role of FDI in achieving national development goals. Short-, medium- and long-term constraints to FDI attraction are highlighted and potential areas for FDI are identified. The proposed strategy elaborates on two scenarios for FDI. The first one assumes a continuation of existing conditions and suggests measures to moderately increase FDI inflows. The second scenario builds on the hypothesis that significant progress has been achieved in mitigating constraints, in particular those related to infrastructure. Under this scenario, the strategy proposes a number of bolder initiatives to improve investment conditions and attract FDI in selected sectors.

Chapter IV highlights the main findings and recommendations of this review.

# CHAPTER I

# FDI TRENDS AND PERFORMANCE

Sierra Leone is a country in transition from post-conflict stabilization to economic rehabilitation and growth. Following 11 years of civil war (1991–2002), which devastated Sierra Leone's social, economic and institutional conditions, political stability has been re-established as reflected in two successful presidential and district-level elections, which included a peaceful transfer of power. During this transformative period, the government has prioritized infrastructure development, reforms to domestic revenue collection and reforms supporting the development of the private sector. To support these priorities, national goals focus on increasing investment, including FDI, in the areas of energy, transport and agriculture.

## A. Economic background

In the 1990s, there was a significant increase in TNCs' investment in developing countries. While many countries were beginning a process of international economic integration and implementing policies to attract FDI, Sierra Leone was consumed by war. Foreign investors, with the exception of few mining companies, largely bypassed Sierra Leone when considering investment opportunities in Africa.

Sierra Leone's war affected the entire country from the eastern border with Liberia, and the diamond mines located there, to the capital city of Freetown in the western part of the country. The Revolutionary United Front's capture of the diamond mines proved to be pivotal because the sale of diamonds provided a steady stream of funding. The war had a high human cost as civilians were targets and were often press-ganged into mining or becoming soldiers. From 1991 to 1999, over 75,000 people were killed, half a million Sierra Leoneans became refugees and 2.25 million people were displaced (half of the population at the time) (Smillie *et al.*, 2000).

The toll on the economy, infrastructure and productive capacity was especially severe given the country's stage of development at the start of the conflict. In the 1980s, before the conflict, economic growth was an annual average of 1.8 per cent. During the war, the formal economy shrank by nearly 40 per cent between 1990 and 1999 (World Bank, 2007a). Rampant corruption connected to the diamond trade had severely weakened public institutions. Unable to withstand further pressure, institutions had collapsed completely by the end of the war. There were several failed attempts to establish a sustainable peace process (1996 Peace Accord, 1999 Lomé Peace Agreement and two Abuja Agreements in 2000). It was only after the second Abuja cease-fire agreement, which was signed in 2001, that hostilities declined significantly and progress was made in disarmament efforts. By January 2002, the government was reasserting its authority, and in the summer of the same year the Truth and Reconciliation Commission and the Special Court for Sierra Leone were established.

The 2002–2008 period brought about significant change although many challenges still remain. The country's political stability was demonstrated during the election in September 2007, when the opposition party's presidential candidate was elected and took office peacefully. While the elections have been fundamental to Sierra Leone's continued development, there has been very limited progress on social issues (i.e. poverty reduction, education and employment), rebuilding infrastructure and institutions, and improving management capacity of general and sector policies. The new administration is seeking to address these issues through a variety of legal reforms and the attraction of FDI.

## 1. Growth and macroeconomic developments

Despite the challenges facing Sierra Leone, recent economic growth has been strong. After an initial post-war surge, economic growth has been sustained at an annual average of 7.6 per cent from 2003 to 2007,

## Figure I.1. Real GDP growth, 1980–2007
### (Per cent)

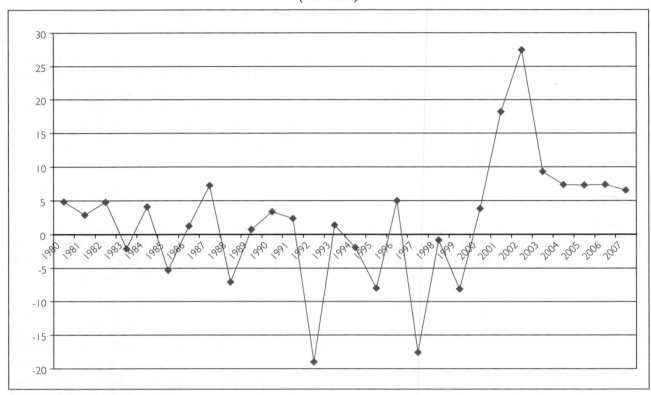

*Source:* World Bank, 2008.

which is the best performance since 1980 (figure I.1). This recovery has been supported by the reactivation of the agricultural and mining sectors and, on a smaller scale, the services sector (transport, communication, trade and tourism). In a comparative context, Sierra Leone's recent growth performance has surpassed the sub-Saharan Africa average (5.7 per cent) and the average of heavily indebted poor countries (5.4 per cent).[1]

Despite the recovery since 2000, real gross domestic product (GDP) per capita is still 20 per cent below the 1980 level (figure I.2). The widening of the gap between the growth of GDP and of GDP per capita is the result of a rapid post-conflict increase in population, which is related, in particular, to the return of about 470,000 refugees during this period (United Nations, 2007). The population growth rate is expected to decline to 2 per cent from 2005 to 2010 and this will help boost GDP per capita if economic growth is maintained.

### a.   Other key macroeconomic variables

In general, Sierra Leone has made an effort to maintain a stable macroeconomic environment, which is critical for FDI attraction. As is typically the case in a fast-growing post-conflict reconstruction period, annual average consumer price inflation rose sharply. By 2004, inflation had reached a high of 14.4 per cent. The government adopted policies focused on reducing inflation, and by 2006 inflation fell to 9.5 per cent. In 2007, inflation in Sierra Leone, as a net importer of food and fuel, began to increase once again, reaching 11.6 per cent due to external shocks affecting the prices of these commodities. The nominal effective exchange rate depreciated enough in 2006–2007 to offset the rise in inflation, keeping the real exchange rate stable and in line with fundamentals, despite the deterioration of terms of trade (International Monetary Fund (IMF), 2008a).

---

[1]  The period of comparison with these countries is from 2004 to 2006.

**Figure I.2. Real GDP and GDP per capita, 1980–2007**
(1980=100)

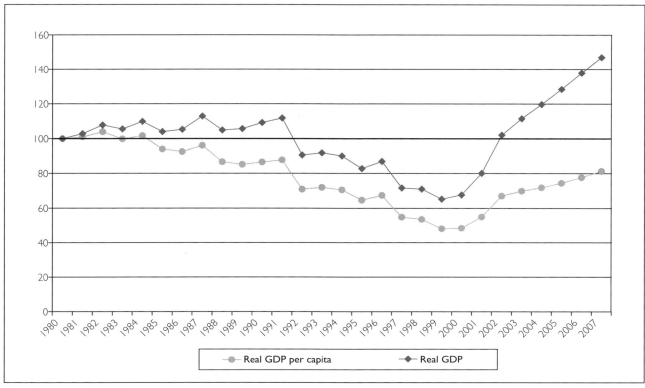

Source: World Bank, 2008.

Domestic tax revenues have continued to fall in the face of a large informal sector and a lack of capacity for tax enforcement. The informal sector represents an estimated 60 to 80 per cent of the economy. In order to cover budget shortfalls, the government relies on grants, which have averaged 40 per cent of government budgetary resources from 2000 to 2005. Also, interest rates and lending have been affected by the shortcomings in revenue generation. Commercial banks' lending rate fluctuated between 24 to 30 per cent in 2006 (IMF, 2008a). Frequent treasury bond auctions held by the Central Bank (usually weekly) pay approximately 18 per cent, causing a crowding out of credit flows to factor and product markets (United Nations, 2008).

## 2.    Structure of the economy

In the 1980s, the economic structure of Sierra Leone was based mainly on domestic activities – agricultural and services sectors – and exports concentrated on few minerals. While there was a burgeoning tourism industry, the 1980s were also marked by a declining trend in the mining sector's contribution to GDP. The structure of the economy has remained relatively unchanged over the post-war period (figure I.3). Agriculture has maintained a central role in the economy followed by the service and industrial sectors respectively. The declining share of the services sector between 2002 and 2006 can be explained by a decrease in tourism and related services as a result of the drawdown of international organizations' staff as the country stabilized after the war (Woody, 2008).

From 2001 to 2006, while the services sector grew at an annual average of 6 per cent, industry (other industry and manufacturing together) and agriculture grew at 14 and 13 per cent respectively. The transport and communication sector as well as the finance and real estate sectors were the main drivers behind the services sector's growth. In the agricultural sector, growth has been mainly in crops and to a lesser extent in fisheries, while in the industrial sector it has been concentrated in mining and construction, compensating

## Figure I.3. Real GDP by sector
### (Per cent)

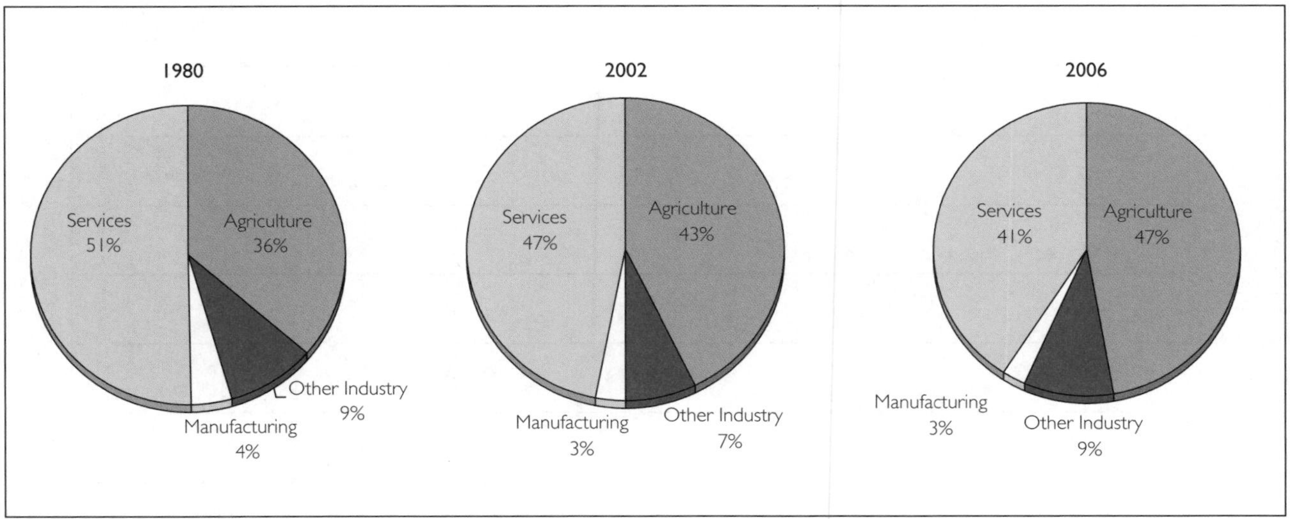

*Source:* UNCTAD Statistics, 2008.

for slow growth in manufacturing. Overall, the structure of Sierra Leone's economy compares with least developed countries (LDCs) as a group and countries in the region.

Given Sierra Leone's rich soil and plentiful rainfall, it is not surprising that agriculture is an essential sector to the economy. Before the war, Sierra Leone was nearly self-sufficient in rice production, its main staple. The displacement of approximately 500,000 farming families between 1991 and 2000 caused overall agriculture production to decrease by 30 per cent from pre-conflict levels and rice production by 20 per cent (United Nations Development Programme (UNDP), 2005a). With the return of many Sierra Leoneans, production is once again increasing. By 2004, rice production had returned to pre-conflict levels and in 2006 had more than doubled compared to 1990 pre-conflict levels (table I.I). Another sign of the sector's ongoing recovery, which is noted later in the chapter, is the 8 per cent annual average decline of rice imports from 2002 to 2007.

## Table I.I. Production of key crops
### (In thousands of tons)

|               | 1990 | 1995 | 2000 | 2003 | 2006  |
|---------------|------|------|------|------|-------|
| Cassava       | 123  | 219  | 241  | 325  | 350   |
| Cocoa beans   | 24   | 10   | 11   | 12   | 14    |
| Coffee, green | 26   | 25   | 15   | 17   | 18    |
| Oil palm fruit| 250  | 225  | 175  | 195  | 195   |
| Rice, paddy   | 504  | 356  | 199  | 446  | 1 062 |

*Source:* Food and Agriculture Organization of the United Nations (FAO) Statistics Division, 2008.

Although the land resource base is broad, with 75 per cent of total land area suitable for cultivation, only 15 per cent is cultivated. Of the cultivated land, only 20 per cent is devoted to cash crops (2.5 per cent of overall arable land), mainly coffee, cocoa and some palm oil (New Partnership for Africa's Development (NEPAD), 2005). Severely hampered by the war and still short of pre-conflict 1990 levels, exports of coffee and cocoa are rebounding; however, moving beyond small-scale farming is proving difficult due to the lack of road infrastructure. The government estimates that approximately 60 per cent of all produce spoils in transit, reflecting the difficulties of transporting goods to markets as well as a lack of capacity for processing and preserving produce. Other challenges include the limited use of technology and technical experience. In this regard, FDI could play a significant role in the transition from small-scale subsistence farming to larger-scale commercial processing for export. However, the barriers of a restrictive land tenure system and the lack of infrastructure need to be addressed for foreign investors to enter the sector.

Non-farming production activities in Sierra Leone are largely concentrated in mining. As early as the 1930s, diamonds and iron ore were discovered and exploited. Subsequent geological surveys revealed that Sierra Leone also possesses platinum, nickel and ilmenite deposits and important endowments of bauxite and gold as well as the world's richest rutile deposit.[2] Indeed, rutile and bauxite exports accounted for an average of 13 per cent of GDP from 1990 until the mines closed in 1995 due to the conflict (Central Bank, 2007). During the same period (1990–1995), diamond exports accounted for only 3 per cent of GDP and their contribution to the economy continues to decline significantly as a result of smuggling and lack of governance.[3]

## Table I.2. Mineral export volumes, 1987–2007

| | Diamonds (thousand carats) | Gold (ounces) | Bauxite (metric tons) | Rutile (metric tons) | Ilmenite (metric tons) |
|---|---|---|---|---|---|
| 1987 | 304.0 | 10 991.0 | 1 279 000.0 | 123 628.0 | - |
| 1988 | 25.0 | 1 425.1 | 1 428 500.0 | 114 300.0 | - |
| 1989 | 131.0 | 7 161.0 | 1 547 100.0 | 141 700.0 | 63 900.0 |
| 1990 | 91.0 | 504.0 | 1 429 400.0 | 141 900.0 | 56 400.0 |
| 1991 | 254.6 | 619.0 | 1 176 800.0 | 143 900.0 | 57 000.0 |
| 1992 | 313.0 | 1 626.0 | 1 365 100.0 | 147 600.0 | 62 500.0 |
| 1993 | 159.3 | 5 059.0 | 944 900.0 | 143 500.0 | 51 900.0 |
| 1994 | 241.3 | 3 557.0 | 734 700.0 | 154 108.0 | 51 700.0 |
| 1995 | 213.6 | 130.7 | - | - | - |
| 1996 | 270.1 | 523.4 | 32 846.0 | 5 924.0 | - |
| 1997 | 69.9 | - | 99 547.0 | - | - |
| 1998 | 15.9 | 22.0 | - | - | - |
| 1999 | 9.3 | - | - | 4 757.0 | 2 614.0 |
| 2000 | 77.5 | - | - | - | - |
| 2001 | 224.4 | 5.8 | - | - | - |
| 2002 | 351.7 | - | - | - | - |
| 2003 | 506.8 | - | - | - | - |
| 2004 | 691.8 | - | - | - | - |
| 2005 | 668.7 | 751.2 | - | - | - |
| 2006 | 582.3 | 2 642.1 | 970 654.6 | 70 361.3 | 8 561.0 |
| 2007 | 604.7 | 6 513.4 | 1 154 223.5 | 86 505.4 | 12 006.0 |

Source: Central Bank of Sierra Leone, June 2008 Statistics.

The closure of the bauxite and rutile mines as well as the civil conflict caused the overall mining sector's contribution to GDP to decline from a high of 20.3 per cent in 1997 to just 5 per cent in 2007. Since 2002, the mining sector has had a strong re-emergence, as the export volumes illustrate (table I.2). Recent developments in mining such as the reactivation of the rutile and bauxite mines in 2006, renewed

---

[2]  Bauxite is used in the production of aluminium; rutile is used primarily for the production of titanium and to create white pigment for paints (titanium dioxide pigment); ilmenite is also used to produce white pigment or titanium dioxide.

[3]  Legitimate diamond exports declined from more than 2 million carats annually by the end of the 1960s (Partnership Africa Canada (PAC), 2004) to 595,000 in 1980 (Hirsch, 2001).

diamond mining and the implementation of the Kimberly Process Certification Scheme[4] for diamonds are having a positive effect on the sector's contribution to the economy. The efforts to bring more diamond exports into official channels have been somewhat successful. From 2003 to 2007, the value of diamond exports reached an annual average of 10 per cent of GDP and in terms of volume, 2007 diamond exports were the third highest recorded since 1987. Renewed mining activities in other minerals such as gold and ilmenite are also beginning to play a factor in mining's overall economic contribution. Current plans to start exploiting iron ore once again will also contribute to the mining sector's recovery and growth. However, sector management and legal conflicts, notably over mining contracts, present and act as a discouraging factor for investment in the sector.

As with much of sub-Saharan Africa, a strong manufacturing sector has been elusive in Sierra Leone. A large informal sector produces handicrafts and furniture while the formal sector is largely comprised of beverages and cement geared towards meeting local market demand. Recently, manufacturing activities were broadened under two Chinese development assistance initiatives. In 2003, the Magabass Sugar Complex was restored and a lease contract was signed between the Government of Sierra Leone and the China National Complete Plant.[5] In 2005, the Henan Guoji Industry and Development Company began to rehabilitate existing structures and develop an industrial trade zone. Plans include locating 15 Chinese factories in the zone. Thus far, they have begun several light manufacturing and processing businesses in the zone including paint, tiles, zinc, oxygen and mattresses.

Outside of these two projects, Sierra Leone has yet to attract foreign investment in the manufacturing sector. The lack of infrastructure, electricity in particular, has been a significant hindrance to the development of this sector. The costs of maintaining a generator or building a dedicated power source often mean that domestic goods simply cannot compete with more competitive imports.

## 3. External sector

In 2006, the current account deficit increased to $112.2 million, representing 8.6 per cent of GDP, slightly above the 8.4 per cent in 2005.[6] This resulted from the deterioration in the services and current transfer balances, which more than offset the gains recorded for the merchandise and income accounts. Net current transfers decreased 53.9 per cent to $63.2 million (Central Bank, 2007). The decrease can partly be attributed to delayed donor support related to missed fiscal targets and the 2007 elections. The services account deficit more than quadrupled to $57.5 million from a deficit of $13.2 million in 2005. The increasing services account deficit is tied to the shipping costs related to increasing imports and construction services.

Sierra Leone has traditionally recorded a trade deficit as a result of its reliance on imports, particularly food and fuel. Reconstruction efforts and the reactivated mining sector have also caused an increase in manufactured goods and machinery imports. The rising cost of fuel imports until November 2008 was the main driver behind the widening trade deficit, reversing the narrower balance since 2003 (figure 1.4). Sierra Leone's gradual reduction in the volume of food imports, particularly rice, slowed the expansion of its trade deficit. By the end of 2008, the sharp reversal of world energy prices should ease the unfavourable terms of trade that the country has dealt with in recent years.

In terms of export value, there has been a considerable surge since 2000 (figure 1.5). By 2007, exports were more than double the 1990 level. As noted earlier, minerals, in particular diamonds, have long been the main exports of Sierra Leone. The increase in exports since 2000 is mostly due to factors such as the ability of the government to migrate diamond exports to official channels, the reopening of the bauxite and rutile

---

[4]  Under the Kimberly Process, diamond shipments can only be exported and imported within co-participant countries in the Kimberly Process. No uncertified shipments of rough diamonds will be permitted to enter or leave a participant's country. In November 2002, 52 governments ratified and adopted the Kimberly Process Certification System, which was fully implemented in August of 2003. Today, 74 governments, in partnership with the diamond industry and non-governmental organizations (NGOs), are committed and legally bound to the United Nations-mandated process (World Diamond Council, 2008).

[5]  The plant produced and exported 8,000 tons of sugar in 2005.

[6]  Current account data were only available from 2004 to 2006.

**Figure I.4. Value of key imports and trade balance** (in millions of dollars)

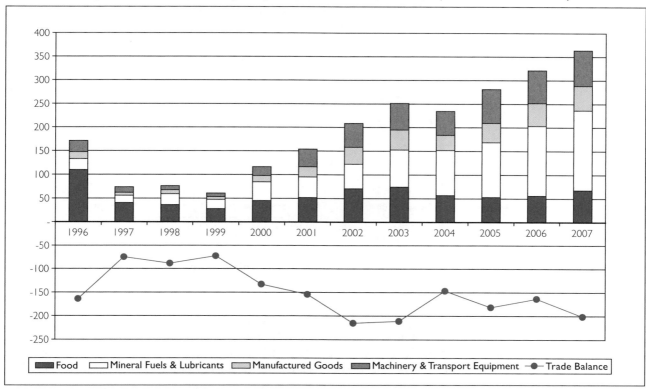

*Source:* Central Bank (2008) and World Bank (2008).

**Figure I.5. Value of total domestic exports** (in millions of dollars)

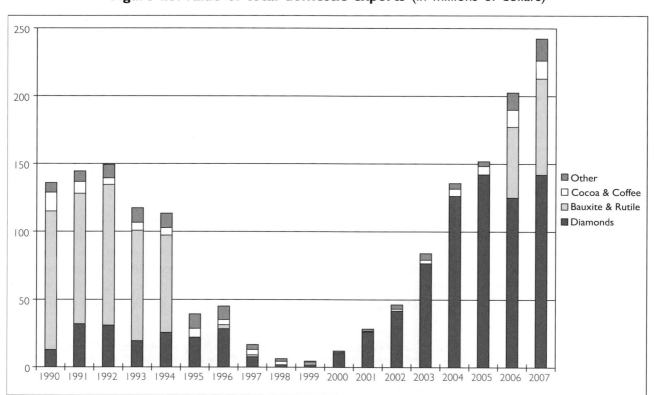

*Source:* Sierra Leone Customs and Excise Department GDD.

**Figure I.6. Sierra Leone coffee and cocoa exports and world market prices, 1997–2007**

(In dollars per ton and United States tons)

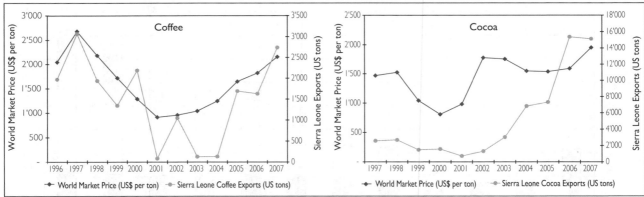

Note: Due to price data availability, exports have been converted from metric tons to United States tons.
*Sources:* Sierra Leone Central Bank, Sierra Leone Customs and Excise Department, International Coffee Organization, International Cocoa Organization.

mines and new industrial[7] diamond mining projects (section B of this chapter – FDI Trends, distribution by sector).

Albeit to a much lesser extent than mining, agriculture is contributing to export earnings once again. In particular, exports of cocoa and coffee, important agricultural exports prior to the conflict, have begun to recover. In 2007, these two commodities together equalled 6 per cent of total export value, 86 per cent of which was from cocoa alone. This recovery occurred during a period of increasing world market prices. The resurgence of these cash crops is a promising development which could contribute, if sustained for a certain period, to the development of rural areas (figure I.6).

### 4. Infrastructure

The lack of supply of electricity, water, roads and telecommunications is a considerable impediment to future development and investment in the country. The limited existing infrastructure deteriorated significantly during the war and the country is particularly challenged by electricity generation and distribution. This poses a serious constraint to attracting FDI (box I.1). Electricity generation, estimated at just under 40 megawatts (MW), falls drastically short of the estimated power requirements, which range from 300 MW to 500 MW for the country.[8] Transmission poses a further challenge in the sense that the network can only bear 46 MW. This is a critical issue that must be addressed rapidly as plans to increase production capacity move forward (e.g. the Bumbuna hydropower plant currently under construction and expected to begin generating power in 2009). Under these capacity constraints, only 2 per cent of households or 40,000 customers (mostly in or near Freetown) have access to electricity (World Bank, 2007b).

Electricity production is primarily petroleum fuelled in Sierra Leone, all of which is imported. In the western region of the country, electricity is generated at the Kingtom and Blackhall Road oil-fired thermal plants. In the Bo and Kenema regions, there is also electrification tied to the mining industry, which comes from both thermal plants and a hydropower plant. The National Power Authority (NPA) was until recently in charge of the generation, transmission, distribution, supply and sale of electricity. A 2006 legal reform opened the sector to private participation (chapter II) and in 2007, through a public-private partnership

---

[7] Until recently, the primary mining method in Sierra Leone was alluvial mining (low capital-intensive, largely non-mechanized). Over the past several years, a more industrial method, kimberlite mining (high capital-intensive, mechanized mining of underground kimberlite pipes) has begun to be used, although alluvial is still the predominant method.

[8] Prior to the civil conflict, Sierra Leone's generating capacity was about 120 MW (CEMMATS Group, 2004). According to an official statement, in November 2007, the electricity requirement for the country was 300 MW (Bangura, 2007). However, the World Bank, based on population growth and current industrialization rate, has estimated that up to 500 MW is required (World Bank, 2006).

---

**Box I.I. The cost of power shortages for investors**

Approximately 70 per cent of power consumption in Sierra Leone is industrial or commercial, yet the lack and cost of electricity is one of the most frequently cited challenges facing investors. Typically, investors have chosen to operate their own generators rather than face frequent power interruptions. One example is Leocem, a cement manufacturer, which has built its own 5 MW power house. Another example is Sierra Rutile, a mining company, which built a new power house containing four 7.5 MW caterpillar generators at a cost of $29 million. Celtel, a mobile phone operator, uses a generator to run the main switch 24 hours a day and places two generators for every tower site in order to maintain 24-hour service. The company also pays for security guards to protect against the theft of the fuel in the generators. Implementing these measures has made Sierra Leone a very expensive place to do business.

*Source:* UNCTAD fact-finding mission, June 2008.

---

agreement, Global Trading Group of Belgium and Income Electrix of Nigeria were permitted to enter the market as generators. Under this arrangement, the NPA maintains control of transmission and distribution. Furthermore, in December 2007, two new generators were installed at the Kingtom Power Plant in Freetown, which has alleviated some of the shortages in the city.

Water systems are overburdened and in need of modernization. In this regard, only 59 per cent of the population have access to safe drinking water and more than half of rural households use contaminated water (UNDP, 2007). The Guma dam, supplying water to Freetown, illustrates the need for infrastructure renewal and maintenance. The dam was intended to supply a population of 500,000, but the influx of people from rural areas, returning refugees and high population growth rates have resulted in a city of 1.5 to 2 million inhabitants. Deforestation has created further problems in the dam region by allowing mudslides, which fill in the dam lake and reduce the available supply.

With respect to road infrastructure, there is need for significant investment. The paved road network is very limited (table 1.3). Of the 11,300 km of roads only 8 per cent was paved as of 2007. In comparison, Ghana has 18 per cent, Ethiopia 12 per cent and Niger 25 per cent.[9] Unpaved rural, feeder roads are also in a serious state of disrepair and as such present a formidable barrier to the development of the agricultural sector. Over the last several years, donor-funded projects have begun to improve and extend the paved roads in Sierra Leone. The European Commission (EC) currently funds over a third of all road rehabilitation (Ministry of Transport and Aviation, 2007). At the end of 2007, a loan agreement was signed between the Government of Sierra Leone and the Organization of the Petroleum Exporting Countries, Kuwait, the Saudi Fund, the Arab Bank for Economic Development in Africa and the African Development Bank for the construction of two highways – one connecting two beach areas (Tokeh–Lumley) and another one leading inland (Kenema–Koidu). As of 2008, 500 km of gravel roads were rehabilitated and 1,200 km of trunk roads had been constructed (IMF, 2008a).

**Table I.3. Road network in Sierra Leone, 2007**

(In kilometres)

| | Paved | Gravel/Earth | Total |
|---|---|---|---|
| Primary | 756 | 1 384 | 2 140 |
| Secondary (gravel) | 24 | 1 880 | 1 904 |
| Feeder roads | 0 | 4 152 | 4 152 |
| Urban roads | 35 | 1 | 36 |
| Local roads and streets | 80 | 2 988 | 3 068 |
| Total length of roads | 895 | 10 405 | 11 300 |

*Source:* Ministry of Transport and Aviation (2007).

---

[9] Figures cited for comparators were reported for 2003, whereas figures cited for Sierra Leone are for 2007 (World Bank, 2008).

Landline telecommunications infrastructure is similarly in a state of deterioration and is a constraint for the operation of FDI projects. The Sierra Leone Telecommunications Company (Sierratel) is the national provider. Currently, there is only one landline per 200 people (table I.4). Of the landlines that are provided, 50 per cent are business lines (National Committee for Privatization (NCP), 2005). Mobile network coverage is increasing; approximately 80 per cent of the country now has cellular coverage. Mobile subscription is growing at a pace that is in line with neighbouring countries and other comparators. Internet usage has also been on the rise, with 5,000 new users from 2000 to 2005, as telecommunications companies widen their scope of investment in the country.

**Table I.4. Telecommunications indicators, 2005**

| | Landlines (per 200 inhabitants) | Mobile subscribers (per 200 inhabitants) | New mobile subscribers 2000–2005 (thousands) | Internet subscribers (thousands) | New Internet users 2000–2005 (thousands) |
|---|---|---|---|---|---|
| Ghana | 2.9 | 25.7 | 2,712.4 | 401.3 | 38.0 |
| Guinea | 0.4 | 4.7 | 112.8 | 50.0 | 28.0 |
| Liberia | 0.4 | 9.7 | 92.9 | - | 1.5 |
| Rwanda | 0.5 | 6.4 | 99.7 | 50.0 | 33.0 |
| Sierra Leone | 1.0 | 4.4 | 101.3 | 10.0 | 5.0 |

*Source:* ITU (2007).

## 5. Social issues

Sierra Leone has always been ranked among the bottom five countries in the UNDP's Human Development Index. Due to the protracted conflict, Sierra Leone is still ranked 180th out of 182 countries in 2009. The destruction the conflict wrought has made it difficult to progress toward reaching the Millennium Development Goals (MDGs). Limited data collection makes the assessment of progress towards the MDGs challenging. As the figures in table I.5 show, progress has been uneven. The number of people living on less than $1 per day has increased slightly;[10] on the other hand, there has been significant progress in universal education. Unfortunately, this has yet to translate into greater literacy. Today, just over one third of the total adult population is literate, a figure that shrinks to 23 per cent among women (UNDP, 2007). Recent efforts to boost enrolment have been successful and, with the high enrolment rates, it is reasonable to expect literacy rates to improve as successive generations complete their education.

Unemployment is another important challenge facing Sierra Leone. Unemployment is at 30 per cent with 50 per cent of the employed population being "self-employed",[11] primarily in agriculture. Paid employment accounts for less than 6 per cent of total employment, with only 2 per cent of women reporting paid employment (UNDP, 2007). Although unemployment is high and gradually increasing (7 per cent to 9 per cent from 2003 to 2007), the absolute number of workers employed is growing much more rapidly, from 64 per cent to 71 per cent over the same period (IMF, 2008b). Of heightened concern is youth[12] unemployment, which, at 55 per cent (UNDP, 2007), is an especially striking figure in a country where 61 per cent of the population is under the age of 24 (United Nations, 2007). As a result of the destabilizing effect of unemployment and youth unemployment in particular, addressing this issue has become a critical component of peacebuilding programmes and of the attraction of foreign investors.

---

[10] It is worth noting that in the IMF's Second Poverty Reduction Strategy (IMF, 2008b), the national asset-based headcount of poverty decreased from 67.5 per cent in 2003 to 61.6 per cent in 2007; the six basis-point drop indicates that progress is being made in the reduction of poverty.

[11] These are survey respondents who identified themselves as "self-employed".

[12] Youth is defined as 15–34 years of age.

### Table I.5. Selected Millennium Development Goals

| | 2000 | 2007 Status | 2015 Target |
|---|---|---|---|
| Halve the proportion of the population living on less than $1 (%) | 57[a] | 59 | 28.5 |
| Universal primary education (% gross enrolment)* | 65 | 109[b] | 100 |
| Reduce by 2/3 the under-five mortality rate (per 1,000 births) | 286 | 270[c] | 95 |

*The figure used for the MDG target (net enrolment) is not available.
[a] 1993.
[b] Greater than 100 because of older re-enrolled students.
[c] 2006.
Sources: UNDP (2005b, 2007).

## 6.  Current policies promoting investment and private sector development

Sierra Leone is carrying out its development strategy under the "National Long-Term Perspectives – Sierra Leone Vision 2025 Programme". The core of this programme revolves around fostering "a strong, self-reliant, and competitive private sector-led economy with strong indigenous participation". Using the overarching strategies set out in the Vision 2025, current macroeconomic policy is being conducted under a Poverty Reduction Strategy Paper (PRSP) developed with the IMF.[13] Aspects of the plan include infrastructure development, reforms to increase domestic revenue collection and private sector development. The PRSP II, published in 2008, puts priority on: (i) energy, (ii) agriculture and fisheries, (iii) transportation and (iv) human development.

Both the Vision 2025 and the PRSP have identified the following as key challenges in the development of the private sector and investment: dominance of a substantial and growing informal subsector; Sierra Leoneans' limited capacity to participate in investment activities; and a weak institutional environment in which small and medium-sized enterprise (SME) growth can be fostered. As part of the effort to address these issues, Sierra Leone is collaborating with various donor agencies on a private sector development programme that has carried out several diagnostic surveys and is now focusing on capacity-building for indigenous SMEs.

A facet of the private sector development effort, which focuses on improving investment (both domestic and foreign), is the privatization programme begun in 2002, which has encompassed more than simply divestiture of government assets. In 2002, the government established the National Commission for Privatization (box I.2). Under the new commission, there is a rigorous review of existing legislation for each of the sectors, some of which have not changed since pre-independence. Through the review and subsequent proposed legislative and regulatory changes, an investment-friendly framework is expected to emerge (chapter II).

Despite Sierra Leone's progress in facing the challenges of building a vibrant private sector, the long civil conflict has affected capital formation. The 11-year halt caused by war is manifested today in most areas and particularly in the lack of administrative capacity, weak institutions, legal conflicts and certain investment disputes, and the lack of managerial-level experience and skills. The government is particularly challenged by the lack of skilled workers as it labours to implement development strategies. To overcome these challenges, it is frequently the case that key policy analysts and advisors are funded by donors for one or two years. When the contract expires, the funds or qualified personnel are not available to fill the breach. Thus, if the reforms for investment and FDI attraction are to be sustainable, there must be sufficient funding of public institutions and increased capacity in public administration.

---

[13] The initial PRSP was developed in 2001 as an interim report. Subsequent revisions have been made to obtain the PRSP II in 2008. Although the IMF publishes the report, it is prepared jointly with the World Bank, public, private and other donor agency stakeholders.

---

### Box I.2. The National Commission for Privatization (NCP)

The NCP developed a strategic plan for the divestiture of public enterprise for 2003 through 2006. During this period, there was a concerted effort to bring all initiatives under the PRSP framework. Accordingly, the NCP adapted the privatization strategy to the PRSP timeframe and developed a strategy that extends to 2010. The NCP's objectives are to:

- Create conditions for private sector-driven economic growth;
- Stimulate domestic and foreign investment;
- Reduce the fiscal burden on the government;
- Refocus government resources;
- Strengthen the quality and coverage of infrastructure while reducing the cost;
- Strengthen the quality and coverage of financial instruments and lower transaction costs and risk premiums.

The NCP has taken the dual approach of introducing privatization while concurrently introducing overall sector reforms. In many cases, irrelevant legislation from pre-independence is still in force. In other instances, regulatory bodies have not been created or are operating under a structure that has not kept pace with the changes in Sierra Leone. The sectors to be privatized are:

- Financial services: three banks and one insurance company;
- Transport: seven enterprises including the airport and port authority;
- Energy: the NPA;
- Water: the Guma Valley Water Company;
- Agriculture: three companies;
- Media: three enterprises;
- Telecommunications: Sierratel;
- Others: postal services, housing, the state lottery.

The NCP has divided the enterprises into two groups. The first group, early privatization, is comprised of enterprises where privatization is a straightforward transaction (e.g. banks). The other categories are those that require additional sectoral reforms. It is the objective of the NCP to complete annually two to five transactions of "early privatization" enterprises and one to two enterprises requiring a sectoral approach.

In 2008, several enterprises were planned to go to tender including Rokel Commercial Bank and Sierra Leone Commercial Bank. Also in 2008, a landlord port strategy was developed and a bill drafted to accommodate such an arrangement. As of December 2008, the privatization of these assets and the port strategy bill had yet to be realized.

*Source:* NCP (2006).

---

## B. FDI trends

The following analysis is intended to provide a perspective of FDI performance in Sierra Leone. Typically, the analysis relies on total FDI inflows as well as flows by sector and origin. These data were not readily available in the case of Sierra Leone. As a result, anecdotal or proxy information such as the Central Bank's balance of payments questionnaire for foreign investors was used. The questionnaire is distributed solely for the purpose of collecting balance of payments information (Central Bank, 2007). Although the questionnaire is not intended as a comprehensive survey of FDI in Sierra Leone, it captures a large proportion of foreign firms and in the absence of more reliable data, provides general characteristics of FDI in Sierra Leone.

### I. FDI size and growth

Historically, there have not been significant FDI flows into Sierra Leone. De Beers was the primary foreign investor from the early 1930s through the mid-1980s, but even that investment was fairly limited due to the low-capital intensity of the type of mining being conducted. The significant decline in mid-1980s can be attributed to the exit of De Beers from Sierra Leone. By 1991, the conflict had largely halted all FDI inflows (figure 1.7). One mining exploration project accounts for the surge in 1995; for 2000 to 2003, investments by telecommunications companies and renewed mining exploration projects raised FDI inflows to levels similar to the best pre-war years. From 2004 to 2007, FDI inflows have soared over previous levels: much of this is due to the reopening of the rutile and bauxite mines and later expansion of projects related to those mines. While FDI inflows continued to increase in sub-Saharan Africa in 2008 in spite of the ongoing financial crisis, they declined from their peak ($94 million in 2007) to $30 million in Sierra Leone.

In relation to regional and developing country averages, Sierra Leone's FDI inflows are considerably lower. Overall, Sierra Leone's FDI inflows as a share of GDP, at 2.4 per cent, were closely aligned with the averages of ECOWAS countries during the period 2001–2005. However, for the same period, FDI inflow per capita for Sierra Leone was considerably lower at $6.5 as compared to ECOWAS ($14.0), LDCs ($15.9) and developing economies ($47.2) (table 1.6). These important differences are not surprising given the relatively short period of time between the end of the war in Sierra Leone and the resumption of economic activity under peace conditions.

## 2.   Distribution by sector

The Central Bank's 2007 balance of payments questionnaire shows that among the larger foreign investors, the majority of firms are concentrated in services, primarily banking and telecommunications. However, there are also accounting, airline and shipping firms (figure 1.8). Foreign firms in the industrial sector are primarily in light manufacturing and mining along with two oil and gas firms.

### Figure 1.7.  FDI inflows 1980–2008
(In millions of dollars)

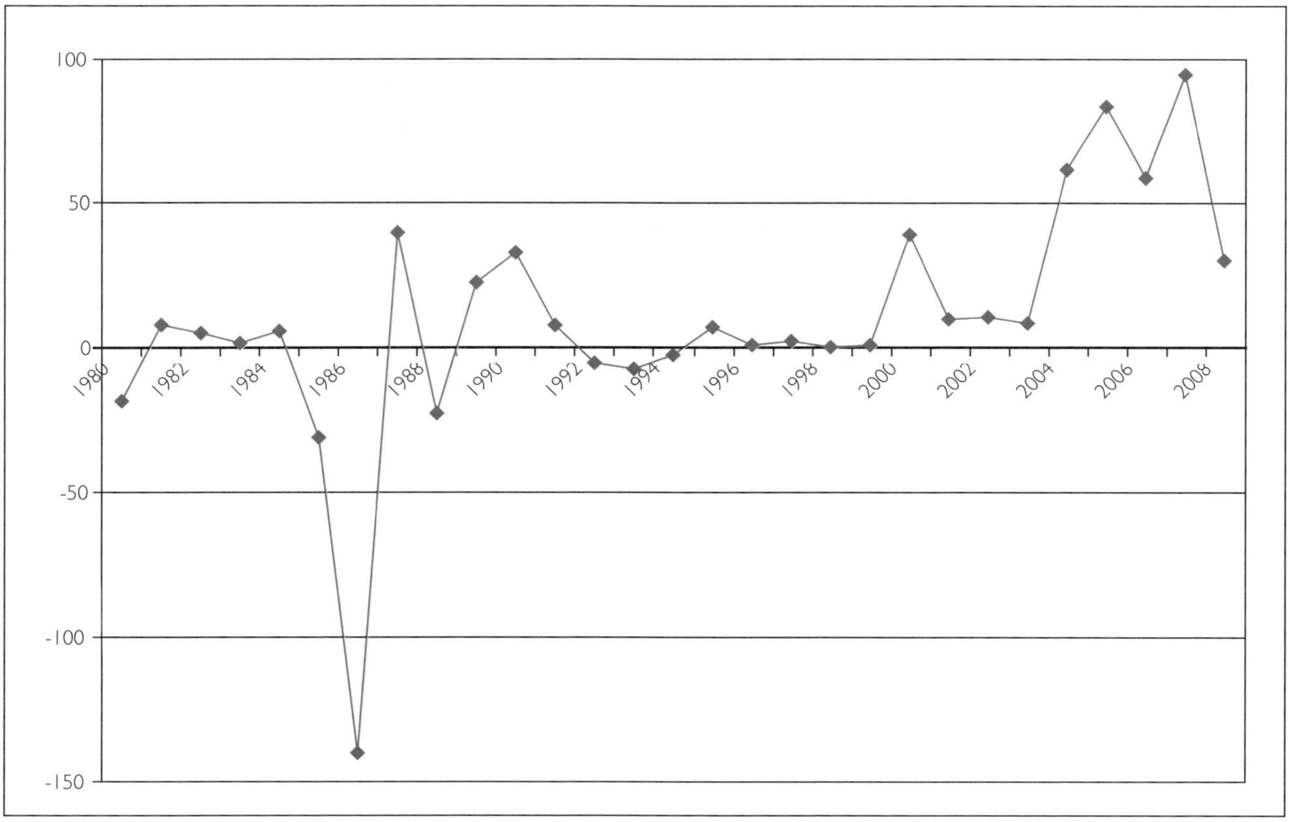

*Source:*  UNCTAD World Investment Report Database (2009).

## Figure I.8. Number of firms by sector

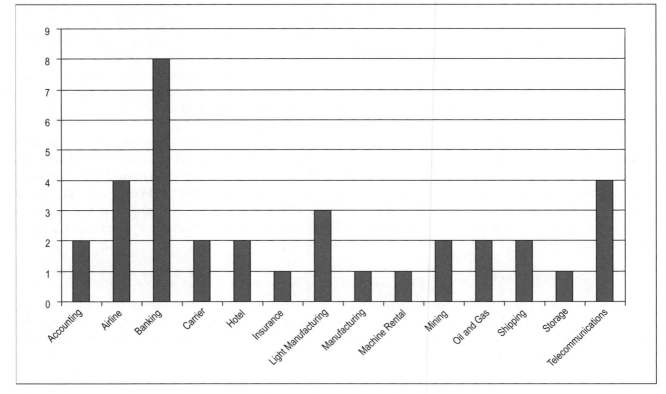

*Source:* Central Bank (2007).

### a. Banking

There are currently 13 foreign-owned commercial banks in Sierra Leone (Central Bank, 2008). The three most recent ones were licensed in September 2008: Skye Bank, Zenith International Bank and the United Bank of Africa. The first foreign bank in Sierra Leone was Standard Chartered from the United Kingdom, which concentrates on business lending. Other banks from Europe include ProCredit (Germany) and International Commercial Bank (Switzerland). The remainder are West African banks from the Gambia, Nigeria and Togo. As the number of foreign-owned banks shows, access to the Sierra Leone banking sector is not restricted. However, the Central Bank encourages foreign banks entering the market to obtain 20 per cent domestic participation.

### b. Telecommunications

Sierra Leone mostly has no fixed line telephony. At the same time, however, mobile telephony is fairly well developed with approximately 80 per cent coverage of the country. At present, there are six mobile telecommunications companies in Sierra Leone, the largest of which is the Kuwaiti firm Zain.[14]

### c. Mining

During the early 1930s, when diamond mining was new to Sierra Leone, De Beers was the first and only mining company. Later, from 1970s until the early 1990s, the industry was nationalized. In the early 1990s, the government attempted to attract new investors to the sector. During this period, as well as in present day operations, the mining sector remains at a fairly non-industrial stage where alluvial mining is the most common mining method and as such is not capital intensive.

---

[14] Other telecommunications firms include Comium (Lebanon), Lintel's Africell (Lebanon), Millicom's Tigo (Luxembourg), Cellcom (Israel) and LAP-Green Networks (Libyan Arab Jamahiriya).

## Table 1.6. Comparative performance of Sierra Leone with selected countries, 1991–2008

(In dollars and percentage)

| Country | Absolute performance | | | | | Relative performance | | | | | | | | | | | | | |
|---|---|---|---|---|---|---|---|---|---|---|---|---|---|---|---|---|---|---|---|
| | Average FDI inflows per year (Millions of dollars) | | | | FDI Stock (Millions of dollars) | Average FDI inflows per year | | | | | | | | | | | | FDI Stock | |
| | | | | | | Per capita (dollars) | | | | Per $1,000 GDP | | | | As per cent of gross capital fixed formation | | | | Per capita ($) | Per cent of GDP |
| | 1991-1995 | 1996-2000 | 2001-2005 | 2006-2008 | 2008 | 1991-1995 | 1996-2000 | 2001-2005 | 2006-2008 | 1991-1995 | 1996-2000 | 2001-2005 | 2006-2008 | 1991-1995 | 1996-2000 | 2001-2005 | 2006-2008 | 2008 | 2008 |
| **Sierra Leone** | **-0.2** | **8.4** | **34.6** | **60.9** | **422.6** | **-0.1** | **1.9** | **6.5** | **10.5** | **-0.4** | **9.0** | **24.2** | **32.4** | **-0.7** | **11.5** | **32.2** | **70.2** | **71.5** | **18.6** |
| Benin | 44.3 | 31.8 | 43.8 | 143.0 | 676.8 | 8.0 | 4.6 | 5.5 | 15.9 | 22.8 | 13.2 | 12.6 | 26.4 | 16.1 | 7.5 | 6.6 | 12.5 | 73.2 | 12.5 |
| Burundi | 0.7 | 2.6 | 0.1 | 0.3 | 48.5 | 0.1 | 0.4 | 0.0 | 0.0 | 0.7 | 3.6 | 0.2 | 0.3 | 0.6 | 4.9 | 0.1 | 0.1 | 5.7 | 4.4 |
| Côte d'Ivoire | 118.4 | 324.6 | 249.1 | 366.1 | 6 054.0 | 8.3 | 20.4 | 14.1 | 19.5 | 11.3 | 27.1 | 18.5 | 17.7 | 11.7 | 19.7 | 19.2 | 21.6 | 317.0 | 25.8 |
| Ghana | 101.4 | 155.8 | 107.6 | 1 203.9 | 5 754.7 | 5.9 | 8.1 | 5.0 | 52.0 | 17.3 | 23.3 | 13.9 | 79.0 | 8.1 | 10.5 | 5.5 | 22.9 | 245.6 | 35.7 |
| Guinea | 12.4 | 26.5 | 63.5 | 620.2 | 2441.2 | 1.9 | 3.3 | 6.9 | 62.4 | 4.0 | 7.1 | 17.9 | 142.1 | 2.1 | 4.4 | 14.9 | 96.0 | 243.6 | 53.7 |
| Liberia | -6.8 | 109.8 | 108.3 | 127.8 | 4 171.5 | -3.4 | 38.7 | 33.5 | 36.9 | -38.6 | 210.9 | 235.7 | 176.3 | -36.1 | 233.1 | 247.9 | 134.2 | 1 170.2 | 499.0 |
| Mauritania | 7.1 | 10.2 | 290.3 | 136.9 | 2 008.4 | 3.3 | 3.9 | 96.8 | 42.3 | 5.4 | 9.4 | 180.5 | 48.9 | 2.9 | 4.5 | 50.2 | 22.6 | 601.7 | 63.5 |
| Mozambique | 32.0 | 178.5 | 258.4 | 389.4 | 3 803.4 | 2.1 | 10.3 | 13.7 | 18.9 | 14.1 | 42.0 | 55.4 | 46.1 | 6.5 | 20.3 | 24.6 | 20.4 | 182.1 | 39.4 |
| Rwanda | 3.6 | 4.4 | 9.6 | 62.0 | 273.7 | 0.6 | 0.6 | 1.1 | 6.5 | 2.0 | 2.4 | 5.0 | 16.0 | 1.3 | 1.5 | 3.1 | 9.0 | 28.3 | 6.1 |
| **ECOWAS** | 1 900.5 | 2 404.3 | 3 529.6 | 19 195.7 | 108 920.1 | 9.8 | 11.0 | 14.0 | 70.1 | 31.5 | 29.9 | 27.6 | 73.4 | 20.6 | 24.3 | 24.6 | 58.7 | 390.3 | 35.3 |
| **Post-conflict group** | 29.4 | 295.3 | 376.4 | 579.5 | 8 297.1 | 1.0 | 8.8 | 9.9 | 13.8 | 5.8 | 39.1 | 48.6 | 41.6 | 3.4 | 22.8 | 26.0 | 19.8 | 194.9 | 51.7 |
| **Least developed countries** | 1 586.1 | 4 170.0 | 11 591.4 | 27 183.2 | 136 167.1 | 2.9 | 6.5 | 15.9 | 34.1 | 11.0 | 24.6 | 48.4 | 62.2 | 6.6 | 13.5 | 24.8 | 30.0 | 167.4 | 25.7 |
| **Developing economies** | 77 905.9 | 202 786.2 | 239 031.0 | 527 947.1 | 4'275 982.0 | 18.0 | 43.1 | 47.2 | 98.8 | 15.7 | 31.1 | 28.7 | 35.6 | 6.4 | 13.1 | 11.6 | 13.0 | 791.2 | 24.8 |

*Source:* FDI/TNC Database (UNCTAD, 2009).

Notes: The post-conflict group comprises Burundi, Liberia, Mozambique and Rwanda.

ECOWAS comprises Benin, Burkina Faso, Cape Verde, Cote d'Ivoire, Gambia, Ghana, Guinea, Guinea-Bissau, Liberia, Mali, Niger, Nigeria, Senegal, Sierra Leone and Togo.

Ultimately, three small mining companies, known as "juniors" and trading on the Canadian stock exchanges, have set up operations in Sierra Leone. Two of them, after several mergers and acquisitions, are still in Sierra Leone today and have launched several new large projects in the country. African Minerals Limited, controlled by the Timis Diamond Company, has been primarily active in alluvial diamond mining. After undertaking extensive and costly surveys for minerals such as iron ore, nickel and uranium, the company has recently discovered kimberlite deposits. Furthermore, in two of its exploration areas in the western and central regions of Sierra Leone, the company has discovered world class iron ore deposits. These findings have prompted plans for more capital-intensive, industrialized mining operations[15] and a $300 million investment in railway and port infrastructure (African Minerals Limited, 2008). This project is however affected by a legal dispute with London Mining Plc due to overlapping rights. Koidu Holdings, a subsidiary of Israeli company Steinmetz Group, is the other junior firm in Sierra Leone. It is significant enough in size to be considered a second-tier competitor to De Beers. As early as 2003, it began more capital-intensive kimberlite mining operations (Koidu Holdings, 2008). The recent transition to capital-intensive kimberlite mining has helped drive the increase in FDI inflows over the last few years.

In addition to diamonds, as noted earlier, the country has significant bauxite and rutile deposits. The Titanium Resources Group Limited, which is owned by a New York hedge fund (Titanium Resources Group (TRG), 2008),[16] reopened the rutile and bauxite mines in 2006. Much of this company's start-up activity is reflected in the surge in FDI inflows in 2004 and 2005. Recently, the company sold its bauxite mining to another junior company, Dutch investment company Vimetco NV, for $40 million (Vimetco, 2008).

Although there are only three mining companies in the production phase, there are a number of companies in the exploration phase for diamonds, gold, iron ore and other base minerals. It is anticipated that several projects will begin operations in the near future, including projects by the African Minerals and London Mining Plc (iron ore) and Cluff Resources (gold). It is estimated that newly built, modern gold and diamond mines planned over the next three to five years could increase mineral export revenues to more than $370 million (Hooge, 2008), an important increase over the $142 million recorded in 2007. New mine construction and refurbishment of older mines can also be expected to attract additional FDI inflows.

In addition to these significant mineral resources, crude oil has been discovered recently off the coast of Sierra Leone by an American company, Anadarko Petroleum Corporation. Although it is too early to assess the magnitude of this discovery, it might present an additional opportunity to attract FDI and generate revenues, which, if carefully managed, could further the development agenda of the country.

## d. Manufacturing

As noted earlier, FDI in manufacturing has entered Sierra Leone primarily under the umbrella of Chinese development assistance projects in 2003 (Magabass Sugar Complex and industrial zone). Investment in manufacturing is largely limited to light manufacturing, beverages (Heineken) and tobacco products for the domestic market. There is one foreign cement manufacturer, Leocem, which was established in 1994. It is a subsidiary of the German company Heidelberg Cement and imports raw materials to manufacture cement. Import tariffs, taxes on fuel, sales tax and miscellaneous fees (chapter II) combined with electricity costs have made exporting cement and manufacturing for domestic consumption unprofitable, and as a result the business focus has shifted away from manufacturing.

## e. Tourism

The tourism sector has been showing signs of recovery and has already attracted some investment from Chinese sources (box I.3). The 5,000 leisure travellers registered in 2005 are far below the 1989 peak

---

[15] Two types of diamond mining occur in Sierra Leone: (1) alluvial mining: low capital-intensive, largely non-mechanized; (2) kimberlite mining: high capital-intensive, mechanized mining of underground kimberlite pipes.

[16] 3 September 2008, commodity hedge fund Ospraie Management LLC, 49 per cent shareholder of TRG closed.

## Box I.3. The tourism sector in Sierra Leone

Sierra Leone has a diverse landscape of mountains, lush vegetation and beaches on a calm ocean, which provides considerable tourism potential. In the 1980s, Sierra Leone's potential was recognized by investors from France – such as Sofitel – and from the United Kingdom. There was air service from a number of European markets, particularly France, available as well. The result was the emergence of a fledgling tourism industry.

Halted by the war, it is now a sector that is once again showing potential. There is ample room for expansion as hotel capacity suitable for tourism is low (approximately 1,000 rooms in 2005). New tourist attractions have recently emerged, particularly in the eco-tourism sector including the Tacugama Chimpanzee Sanctuary, the wildlife research project at Tiwai Island and the Outamba Kilimi National Park. Although the number of tourists is around only 1,000 per year, establishing these attractions highlights the potential for growth in the sector.

A comparison with neighbouring countries' expenditures by international visitors (chart below) shows the potential of tourism in Sierra Leone. Although the majority of tourism in these countries is primarily business travel and visiting friends and family, the figures illustrate that Sierra Leone can improve its overall performance in the sector. The Gambia, a country with about 500 km of coastline, receives over 100,000 leisure tourists per year, mostly from package tours from the United Kingdom and Benelux markets. Comparatively, Sierra Leone has three times the distance of coastline, much of which is undeveloped.

### 2008 estimated international visitor expenditures

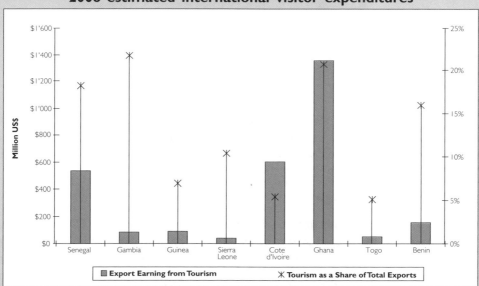

A study of the potential of tourism in Sierra Leone using statistics collected from 2005 illustrates the magnitude of what could happen if the country were to increase accommodation by only 600 rooms. Foreign exchange earnings could double from the $20 million recorded in 2005 to $41 million. An additional 1,800 jobs could be created and local incomes could be expected to more than double from $12 million in 2005 to $25 million in 2015.

Recent investment has come from two Chinese firms under the umbrella of assistance projects. The first, in the early 2000s, came from the Beijing Urban Construction Group, which signed a lease contract with the government to rehabilitate and operate the 11-acre Bintumani Hotel. After a $10 million investment, the hotel opened in 2003. The second involved an agreement between Henan Guoji Investment Development Company (investors in the industrial zone described earlier) and the government to build a 121-acre resort area on reclaimed wetlands near Lumley Beach. Current plans include 8,600 residential units

*Sources:* Embassy of China (2004); McEwen and Siaffa (2005); Stellenbosch University (2005);
    World Resources Institute (WRI) (2003).

### Figure I.9. Firms by origin in Sierra Leone

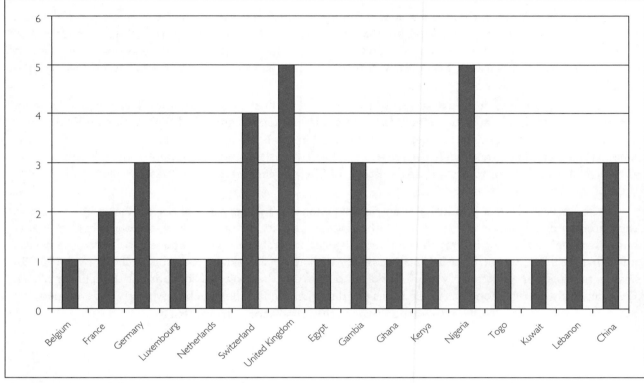

*Source:* Central Bank (2007).

of over 13,000 (Horwath Consulting, 1990). British Airways and Brussels Airlines have started flying back to Sierra Leone with regular direct flights from London and Brussels to Freetown. This is likely to foreshadow new opportunities.[17] Nevertheless, the country's ability to develop its infrastructure, mainly transportation and energy, will remain key factors in boosting the sector.

### f. Other potential sectors for FDI

Although the sectors set out above depict the current primary sectors for FDI, other sectors have FDI potential. This will be particularly the case over the medium and long run if the significant existing impediments are addressed. These other sectors include power generation, maritime transport and construction. In addition, if infrastructure constraints become less problematic and the regulatory environment becomes more investor-friendly, fishing and agro-processing could also present attractive opportunities.

### 3. Distribution of FDI and countries of origin

In general, FDI is concentrated in Freetown, where there is relatively more infrastructure, and in the three major mining areas – Kono and Kenema (in the west for diamonds) and Bonthe (in the south for rutile and bauxite). The remainder of the country has not attracted FDI so far.

The top investors in Sierra Leone are the mining and telecommunications firms, whose origins are fairly diverse (figure I.9). Nigerian investment has a large presence in the banking sector but the amount of FDI is limited. As noted earlier, recent investment from China has been in light manufacturing and tourism.

---

[17] From 1986 to 1989, leisure travellers to Sierra Leone increased at an average annual rate of 25 per cent (Horwath Consulting, 1990).

## C.  Impact of FDI

In Sierra Leone, not only have FDI inflows been relatively low, but there is also a lack of data collection and limited statistics on FDI. This makes it particularly difficult to properly assess and quantify the impact of FDI on the social and economic development of the country. As a result, anecdotal information has been used to provide indications of areas where the presence of FDI is affecting – positively or negatively – the economy or development, but not necessarily to determine the magnitude of its impact. Reviewing statistical methods in order to improve their reliability, frequency and the availability of FDI data would improve the ability to evaluate its impact and the government's ability to formulate FDI attraction strategies.

### 1.  Infrastructure

FDI has contributed significantly to infrastructure improvements in the telecommunications sector. As noted earlier, foreign telecommunications firms have installed a mobile network infrastructure that now provides coverage to 80 per cent of the territory. These companies are installing modern technology and expanding into other areas such as Internet service.

Mining has also contributed to infrastructure improvements, mainly in transport networks through the construction of private facilities. New investment is being committed to rehabilitate infrastructure that has deteriorated during the conflict and post-conflict period. One example is the project of African Minerals ($300 million) to rehabilitate the Pepel Port and loading facilities, the Pepel to Marampa railway line (a line that has not been operational since the 1970s) and the construction of a new railway line to Tonkolili (African Minerals, 2008).

### 2.  Technology and skills

Although there have been only a few FDI projects implemented in Sierra Leone, there has been significant investment in capital equipment in the mining and telecommunications sectors, which has been accompanied by a demand for skilled labour. Recent investment in light manufacturing and tourism is also creating a need for workers with a specific set of skills. Unfortunately, the education and skills of the labour force in Sierra Leone are insufficient to meet demand. Foreign firms have made efforts to solve the problem through training programmes. For example, the mobile telecommunications company Zain has attempted to boost its human resource capital through its Celtel Academy, a school focused on business administration. The mining firms that have been in the country for several years also provide training to their employees. For the most part however, companies rely on expatriates to fill highly skilled and salaried positions.

### 3.  Employment and linkages

Little data are available on employment; however, there have been several assessments of the impact of various foreign firms on employment in Sierra Leone. Due to the labour intensity of the primarily alluvial mining projects in place, it is likely that the mining firms are the largest employers among foreign firms. The Titanium Resource Group reports over 2,000 employees while Koidu Holdings reports approximately 600 employees. Total employment is significantly below pre-war levels, but the World Bank estimates the mining sector could create around 38,000 jobs in the medium term, a figure that would indirectly impact 300,000 people (dependants and extended families).[18] Given recent performance and investment levels in the mining sector, this figure could reach 500,000 by 2020 if additional investment were made in the various mining projects already in place in the country (Adam Smith International, 2007).

There is an overall lack of linkages between FDI and domestic businesses. There seems to be some level of activity by local firms providing services such as transport or printing to foreign firms, but such

---

[18] Conditions listed by the World Bank to bring about greater economic impact from mining include 20–30 private operators in both mining and exploration by 2010 and $15–$30 million investment annually by 2010 (World Bank, 2005).

---

### Box I.4. Sorghum value chain development in Sierra Leone

In 2005, the European Cooperative for Rural Development (EUCORD) and the Heineken subsidiary Sierra Leone Brewery participated in a project to promote a supply chain between domestic sorghum farmers and the brewery.

Sierra Leone imports barley primarily from the United States and Canada but the costly and long supply chain combined with climbing grain prices have made the use of locally produced sorghum an attractive alternative. The five-year programme with a budget of $2.9 million involved 2,000 farmers and focused on:

- Introducing high yielding, high quality sorghum varieties;
- Establishing sorghum collection centres;
- Forming and training village-level producer associations and credit groups;
- Assisting reliable producer groups in entering into longer-term partnerships with the beverage industry;
- Training private sector input dealers in supplying inputs to sorghum farmers through market mechanisms.

This market-led strategy has not only increased the competitiveness of sorghum compared to imported barley but has also, according to a 2006 impact study, increased household income by approximately 10 per cent for the poor and 3.5 per cent for the very poor (unable to afford food).

It should be noted that before the programme, the Sierra Leone Brewery was already generating benefits for the community. It is a top employer in the city of Freetown, employing approximately 175 people in 2006. The same study, which noted the benefits of the sorghum project for the poor, also found that each job at the brewery has in turn generated eight jobs in agriculture and 32 in distribution.

*Sources*: Financial Times (2008); EUCORD (2005); National Committee for International Cooperation and Sustainable Development (NCDO) (2006).

---

connections remain at best tenuous. While there is willingness on the part of foreign firms to engage local businesses (box I.4), the characteristics of local firms make this option less attractive than outsourcing to firms outside the country. One of the most cited problems preventing linkages is supply capacity. Many of the local firms are small and do not have the capacity either in terms of manpower or equipment to supply foreign firms. Another issue is the informality of the local business sector. In the current tax and business registration environment, many firms operate without formal registration, making them both unattractive to foreign firms from a legal aspect and difficult to identify as potential suppliers from a practical perspective.

## 4.   Environment

The mining sector is currently the primary attractor for FDI in Sierra Leone, and while it creates benefits for the economy, these come with certain environmental costs. Rutile mining, for example, is conducted by dredging artificial ponds or lakes. Once an area is mined, the dredging moves to another location, leaving ponds, partially submerged bars of land and inert by-products behind. TRG, the owner of the rutile mines, is in the early stages of several initiatives to address these issues including replanting the bars and aqua-culture. Diamond mining, whether kimberlite or alluvial, also has a significant impact on the environment, including land degradation and pollution or muddying of rivers and streams. Sierra Leone has adopted environmental protection laws to regulate the effects of mining on the environment. However, it is too soon to assess their effectiveness because they are in the early stages of implementation and enforcement capacity is very limited (chapter II).

Outside of mining, Sierra Leone's environment can also be expected to come under pressure from other activities. In this regard, development related to the tourism industry could become a source of concerns. Effectively, the 121-acre resort project that will use wetlands near Lumley Beach has already raised questions about the potential impact on the ecosystem and the environment overall.

**Figure I.10. Destinations of exports, 1984 and 2006**
(Percentage of total export value)

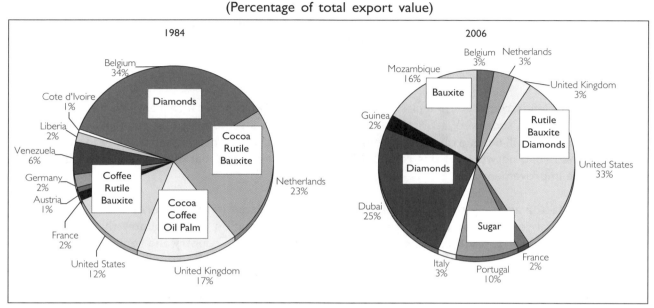

*Source:* UNCTAD and Ministry of Trade and Industry.

## 5. Trade integration

### a. Diversification of exports

The composition of Sierra Leonean exports has remained largely unchanged; minerals, coffee and cocoa remain the primary exports. Recent mining projects in minerals such as gold and iron ore may broaden the spectrum of exported minerals, although export levels are anticipated to remain small in comparison to exports of diamonds, rutile and bauxite. Plans by African Minerals to start mining iron ore (estimated at over 2 billion tons over 40 to 60 years) is one example. In terms of agriculture, although coffee and cocoa are enjoying resurgence, the production of these commodities does not benefit from foreign investment.

### b. Export destination

In 1984, Sierra Leone's exports, primarily bauxite and rutile and to a lesser extent diamonds, cocoa and coffee, were destined for Belgium (34 per cent), the Netherlands (23 per cent), the United Kingdom (17 per cent) and the United States (12 per cent) (figure I.10). Only 3 per cent of exports were directed to African countries. By 2006, exports had shifted away from Belgium. The share of exports to the United States increased considerably to 33 per cent. This increase is due largely to bauxite, rutile and diamond exports. At the same time, the share to Belgium, the Netherlands and the United Kingdom has decreased to about 3 per cent. New destinations that are gaining a significant share of Sierra Leone's exports are Dubai (25 per cent) and Portugal (10 per cent). Diamonds are the major export to Dubai. In the case of Portugal it is sugar from the newly rehabilitated Magabass sugar plant that is being exported. Within Africa, although exports have increased, they are primarily directed towards Mozambique (16 per cent) as bauxite exports.

## D. Assessment

Sierra Leone has made significant progress since peace was declared in 2002. In the seven years after the end of the conflict, Sierra Leone has not only achieved peace and stability but has embarked on an ambitious programme of reconstruction and growth. Its success in reconstruction and future development will depend on its ability to achieve and maintain high levels of growth, to reduce poverty and create jobs, particularly for youth. In each aspect, FDI could play a significant role in moving Sierra Leone closer to its economic, social and political development goals.

The effectiveness of government policies and donor programmes has been hindered by a lack of human resources, capital and capacity. This has affected the speed with which policy changes have been adopted for private sector development, FDI attraction, specific sectoral goals and regulatory reforms in areas such as telecommunications, mining, tourism and fisheries. The focus and priority the government will place on capacity- and institution-building in areas such as regulatory agencies and the judicial system will be key to the future attractiveness of Sierra Leone to investors.

The lack of infrastructure, particularly electricity and transport, poses a challenge to the attraction of foreign investors. The success of attracting FDI to other potential sectors such as tourism, manufacturing and agro-processing will depend on the government's ability to supply uninterrupted power and a reasonably well-maintained road network. In this regard, FDI in the mining sector has already contributed to some infrastructure improvements.

Another factor affecting the elusiveness of FDI is the outdated image of Sierra Leone as a country in conflict. Several years of peace have brought about a transformation in the country that has not been sufficiently publicized and, if addressed, could improve the image of the country and generate interest.

Sierra Leone's valuable mineral resources are finite and as such cannot be expected to continue as its sole source of wealth. Furthermore, commodity cycles are a reality of the global economy and therefore a sound approach is diversity within sectors, where potential exists. As the government works to further develop the mining sector, not only does it need to strike the crucial balance between creating an attractive climate for foreign mining companies and extracting economic benefits from the sector, but it will also need to foster diversity of investment projects in the mining of less traditional Sierra Leonean minerals.

Sierra Leone is faced with myriad challenges, all of which need to be addressed in the near term. The government is working to formulate strategies and move forward with implementation but is frequently faced with disjointed and uncoordinated strategic solutions. At times, this has overwhelmed the already stretched capacity of the government. In an effort to prioritize and implement programmes in a more coherent and consistent manner, Sierra Leone is shifting to a comprehensive strategic approach that integrates the range of various donor- and government-sponsored programmes.

The small but increasing FDI trend since 2003 suggests that there is renewed interest in Sierra Leone as a destination for FDI. It should be expected, however, that FDI inflows remain low. The challenge in the years to come is to improve infrastructure and institutional capacity, and to put in place an effective long-term development and FDI strategy. For implementing a successful FDI strategy and benefiting from its development potential, FDI needs to be incorporated as a key element in the various development strategies (e.g. PRSP II, private sector development, sectoral development).

# CHAPTER II

# THE INVESTMENT FRAMEWORK

Sierra Leone is putting in place one of West Africa's most ambitious reform agendas, which includes investment-related issues. The objectives are to improve the country's investment framework and attract FDI to revitalize economic development. After a number of years of stability and peace, substantial investment-related reforms (annex 1) have been made. In this context, chapter II reviews Sierra Leone's policy framework for investment and provides recommendations to improve it.

As a consequence of the reforms implemented and those in progress, an open FDI regime is in place. Reforms are not complete, however. Furthermore, the effective implementation of new legislation and procedures is an issue the Government of Sierra Leone needs to address. At present, critically needed institutional, financial and human capacity to implement the changes is lacking.

The overall reform, development, consolidation and codification of the legal system in Sierra Leone have been entrusted to the Law Reform Commission appointed in 2003. This commission coordinates these changes with the support of donors. Programmes by the World Bank through the Foreign Investment Advisory Service (FIAS) and the United Kingdom's Department for International Development (DFID), among others, have helped the government focus on reducing procedural barriers, updating and/or drafting laws and introducing fiscal and sector reforms. The continuation and coordination of these efforts, in line with national development policy objectives, are essential to create a good investment climate.

## A.  Entry and establishment of FDI

Sierra Leone has an open legal regime for the entry and establishment of foreign investment. The few remaining limitations on the right of entry are in the services sector. The instances where foreign investors can be subjected to limitations include the commercial presence of foreign entities in a range of professional services, auxiliary transport, internal waterway and rail transport and qualifications for establishing an insurance firm or a bank. The restrictions can take various forms including partnerships, joint ventures, minimum assigned capital or years in business (table II.1).

In practice, it is difficult to identify whether and how the partnership requirements are implemented. Also, it is unclear which entity is responsible for verifying and approving these arrangements. This creates uncertainty for investors. A comprehensive list of restrictions is available from Sierra Leone's schedule in the World Trade Organizations' (WTO) General Agreement on Trade in Services (GATS) (WTO, 1995a).

While these requirements apply to foreign investors, Sierra Leone offers more favourable treatment (full national treatment) to nationals from the Mano River Union[19] and ECOWAS member countries (see the final list of the GATS article II most favoured nation exemptions in WTO, 1995b).[20] For example, in the road transport sector (passengers and freight), only the vehicles registered in the Mano River Union and ECOWAS are allowed to provide services in Sierra Leone. ECOWAS provisions note that each member State accords non-discriminatory treatment to nationals and companies of other member States. If, however, for a specific activity, a member State is unable to reciprocate national treatment, other member States are not bound to accord non-discriminatory treatment.

---

[19] The union is composed of Côte d'Ivoire, Guinea, Liberia and Sierra Leone.

[20] Given that there are no market access schedules for services in the ECOWAS Treaty, it is unclear if these provisions are operational, in particular since national treatment is not formalized in the national law.

While the preferential access granted to regional partners (Mano River and ECOWAS) promotes the important goal of regional integration, in practical terms, limited investment and economic activity has been generated through this discriminatory treatment. Sierra Leone may wish to consider removing these obstacles that affect investment flows from diverse sources and consolidating multilaterally the liberalization of trade in services that has been granted to regional partners.

The Investment Promotion Act (IPA) of 2004 provides the basic legal regime for investment. Article 4 states that any investor, domestic or foreign, may invest in any legitimate form of business. The IPA does not contain any list of sector limitations to FDI entry. Article 3 notes that in addition to the IPA, there are other laws with special provisions to promote investment in tourism, fisheries, mines and minerals, banks, non-bank financial institutions and other business activities that apply to FDI entry (section on taxation).

### Table II.1. FDI entry restrictions in services

| Sector | Current restrictions |
| --- | --- |
| Professional services | The commercial presence of foreign professional services in Sierra Leone requires a partnership with Sierra Leoneans. |
| Other business services | To establish a business service enterprise, a foreign firm has to establish joint ventures with Sierra Leonean partners. |
| Insurance and insurance-related services | For establishing a foreign insurance firm (commercial presence), a firm must: (i) have over 10 years' practice and (ii) hold a minimum assigned capital twice that of local firms. A "letter of comfort" from the parent supervising authority may be requested to provide funds in cases of shortfalls in solvency or liquidity. |
| Banking and other financial services (excluding insurance) | For the right to establish commercial presence in Sierra Leone, it is required that reciprocity treatment be given to a Sierra Leonean firm to establish a commercial presence in a foreign country (e.g. assurance from the parent supervisory authority). Branches of foreign incorporated banks are required to hold a minimum assigned capital twice that of minimum paid-up capital prescribed for locally-incorporated banks. |
| Health and social services | For commercial presence, foreign service providers must be registered practitioners in the appropriate disciplines with qualifications recognized by the Ministry of Health. |
| Internal waterway transport | The commercial presence has to take the form of a joint venture with Sierra Leoneans. |
| Rail transport services | The commercial presence has to take the form of a joint venture. |
| Transport auxiliary services (e.g. customs house brokers) | The commercial presence has to take the form of a joint venture with Sierra Leoneans. |

*Source:* UNCTAD elaboration based on Sierra Leone's WTO commitments under GATS.

While the restrictions to FDI entry in banking, insurance and transport services are common, the partnership requirement in business and professional services acts as an impediment to the goal of capitalizing on the opportunities that the services sector offers to Sierra Leone.

In addition to restrictions on services activities, other entry limitations apply to maritime and airport services. Foreign persons or firms are prohibited from holding licences for the activities of clearing or forwarding air or sea freight cargo operations (article 7 of the Cargo Clearing and Forwarding Act of 1974). Private investors, foreign or domestic, cannot participate in other maritime port activities given that the Sierra Leone Ports Authority (SLPA) has exclusive responsibility for provision of port services (cargo handling and pilotage). SLPA is currently the sole stevedore licensed to operate in the Port of Freetown. Private investors, domestic or foreign, are limited also from participating in airport services as the Sierra Leone Airport Authority Act (1988) grants to the Authority the right to operate and manage Freetown Airport commercial operations.

## B.   Treatment, protection and institutional responsibility for promotion of FDI

### 1.   Treatment and protection

Neither the Constitution nor the IPA of 2004 makes reference to fair and equitable treatment of foreign investors or to a minimum level of treatment. This international law standard is often found in investment treaties, but Sierra Leone has not concluded many. However, this standard is to be handled with care outside and even within the international framework for investment, as the content and the level of protection are not clearly defined and may go beyond the level of protection of physical property or protection against denial of justice that Sierra Leone can currently guarantee.

Three key elements of protection are sought by foreign investors in an FDI regime: protection against expropriation; dispute settlement; and free transfer of funds. Sierra Leone's FDI framework addresses each of these issues in the following manner.

**Protection against expropriation:** Chapter III article 15 of the Constitution is a direct but succinct statement to protect every person from "deprivation of property". A further reference is found in chapter III, article 21(1), which states that "no property of any description shall be compulsorily taken possession of, and no interest in or right over property of any description shall be compulsorily acquired", except for defence, public safety, public order, public morality, public health, town and country planning, or for the promotion of the public benefit or the public welfare. The 2004 Investment Promotion Act further provides that "no private investment, whether domestic or foreign, shall be expropriated or nationalized in a direct or indirect manner, except in the special cases specified by section 21 of the Constitution". The criteria noted above represent a broadly defined list of motives and although these provisions provide a general basis limiting expropriation, discretionary potential exists under the "promotion of the public benefit or the public welfare", creating unpredictability in the investment framework.

The constitutional provisions require prompt payment of adequate compensation, although there is no definition of adequate compensation. Provisions also exist for access to the courts or an independent authority for the determination of rights, the legality of action and the amount of compensation. These provisions follow principles of international law regarding the lawfulness of an expropriation. However, neither article 15 nor article 21 of the Constitution mentions the condition of non-discrimination in the procedure of deprivation of property and compensation.

**Dispute settlement:** Following international standards, the 2004 IPA provides that where a dispute arises between an investor and the government with respect to an investment in a business enterprise or with respect to an investment obstructed or delayed by the government, the parties will use their best efforts to settle such dispute amicably (article 16). The IPA further establishes in the event that such a dispute is not settled amicably, it may be:
  •  Submitted to the United National Commission on International Trade Laws in accordance with the rules of procedure for arbitration;
  •  Pursued within the context of a ratified bilateral or multilateral investment agreement;
  •  Submitted to any other national or international machinery for the settlement of investment disputes as the parties may agree.

Since 1965, Sierra Leone has been a party to the Convention on the Settlement of Investment Disputes between States and Nationals of Other States Party. Although no specific reference is made to the International Centre for Settlement of Investment Disputes (ICSID) Convention, the current provision of the 2004 IPA allows recourse to arbitration under this mechanism for foreign investors. As of 2008, no international dispute involving the Government of Sierra Leone and foreign investors had been submitted for international arbitration.

**Free transfer of funds:** The 2004 IPA provides guarantees for the free transfer of funds with no restrictions on the repatriation of earnings, profits and capital and loan payments. This includes: expatriates' remittances; repatriation of profits (after taxes); proceeds from the liquidation of a business enterprise; awards resulting from any settlement of disputes in business enterprises; and repayments of principal and interest on loans contracted abroad.

Another element related to treatment of investors is access to investment incentives. In the case of Sierra Leone, they are all (foreign and domestic) treated in the same manner. Sectoral laws make, in general, no significant distinction between foreign and domestic investors. De facto national treatment is granted (see the section on taxation for additional information).

## 2. International investment framework

Sierra Leone is lagging behind in the conclusion of international investment treaties compared to most countries in the region. It has signed only three bilateral investment treaties (BITs) – one with Germany (1965), one with the United Kingdom in 1981 that was revised in 2000 and one with China in 2001. The key provisions of the BIT with the United Kingdom, which entered into force in 2001, are:
- Nationals or companies are accorded fair and equitable treatment and enjoy full protection and security.[21] Unreasonable or discriminatory measures are prohibited;
- Investor-state disputes may be referred to ICSID;
- No party grants treatment less favourable than that which it accords to its own nationals or companies or to nationals or companies of any third state;
- Investments cannot be nationalized or expropriated except for a public purpose on a non-discriminatory basis and against prompt, adequate and effective compensation.

In order to close the gap and create a more conducive environment for investment, the current policy of promoting FDI from different sources should target the negotiation of BITs with countries that have the potential to become important sources of FDI.

Sierra Leone is starting with nearly a blank slate and is not, unlike many countries in the region, confronted with inconsistencies between national and international FDI frameworks. It is therefore advisable to ensure a coherent approach between the guarantees and protection given at the national level and those that would be negotiated in the context of new BITs or other investment instruments. International investment law has been subject to many changes and interpretations in recent years. This constitutes an opportunity for Sierra Leone to prepare a consistent and state-of-the-art investment treaty model that takes into account its priorities and specific level of development. Furthermore, an approach combining the negotiation of BITs and double taxation treaties (DTTs), including investment chapters in regional trade agreements, should be used to boost Sierra Leone's FDI attractiveness. These treaties should target key partners, including those with a sizable diaspora such as the United States.

In the ongoing negotiation of the Economic Partnership Agreement with the European Union (EU), the African Conference of Trade Ministers adopted the position that investment should be kept outside

---

[21] The treaty accords fair and equitable treatment and full protection and security; neither party can in any way impair by unreasonable or discriminatory measures the management, maintenance, use, enjoyment or disposal of investments.

the negotiations. While this is an understandable negotiating position, the lack of investment provisions may represent an important missed opportunity to consolidate a favourable investment context including ensuring national treatment, liberalization of investment restrictions and facilitation of BITs and DTTs.

## 3. Institutional responsibility for promotion of FDI

The Investment Promotion Act of 2004 assigned the Sierra Leone Export Development and Investment Corporation business facilitation duties.[22] In 2007, it was replaced by the Sierra Leone Investment and Export Promotion Agency (SLIEPA) to promote investment and export development.

SLIEPA was organized to focus on investment and export development and business facilitation. It receives support from DFID, the International Trade Centre (ITC), the World Bank and FIAS to fund personnel and put in place basic operating conditions, including its structure and work programme.

The mission of SLIEPA focuses on providing personalized services and information to investors and exporters. SLIEPA has identified sectors – agriculture, marine resources, mining, and tourism – for strategic promotion of FDI, while export promotion deals with agriculture and marine resources.

Given the government's current reform agenda and the numerous initiatives to introduce investment-related legal, policy and institutional changes, SLIEPA could play an important role in this process in terms of policy advocacy. This issue is discussed in detail in chapter III.

## 4. Assessment and recommendations on entry, treatment and protection of FDI

Sierra Leone has an open and liberal regime for foreign investment. The 2004 IPA is inspired by best international practices and provides an enabling framework for FDI. Its provisions have an open and liberal approach and it does not contain sector restrictions. To further improve the framework, it is recommended that Sierra Leone guarantee national treatment of FDI by formalizing it in the law. Specific sector laws and other legal provisions do however contain a few restrictions, mostly in services activities. To fully open the investment regime, these restrictions should be removed and Sierra Leone should consider consolidating, at the multilateral level, the liberalization of trade in services that it has granted to regional partners.[23] Finally, it is recommended that Sierra Leone prepare an investment treaty model that should provide the basis to negotiate BITs.

## C. General measures for regulating business

### 1. Enterprise law and corporate governance

Although improvements have been made in Sierra Leone in recent years, establishing a business still involves numerous and time-consuming requirements for registering, obtaining operating licences and seeking approvals from various public entities. The negative effects of these obstacles on doing business are compounded by the lack of clear and transparent regulations and procedures, poor coordination with tax registration and administration, the limited use of computers and the lack of administrative services outside of Freetown.

Recent changes aimed at simplifying business registration have been made through the Investment and Export Promotion Agency Act (2007) and the Registration of Business Act (2007). In addition, the General Law (Business Start-up) (Amendment) Act of 2007 abolished the requirement for foreign investors to obtain

---

[22] To facilitate obtaining registry, permits, licenses, certificates/clearances and identifying joint venture partners.

[23] Sierra Leone used to be an attractive educational centre for students from countries in the region. Investment in educational services could re-establish this tradition in certain technical programmes including the English language.

permission for foreign exchange transactions.[24] The Bankruptcy Act (2009) has made it easier to close a business, thus leading to an enhanced entrepreneurial environment. However, while the 2007 Registration of Business Act simplified some of these procedures, it did not repeal or establish direct links to similar issues (for example registration) defined in the Companies Act.

To establish a business, a number of procedures are required. These procedures apply equally to domestic and foreign investors and are fairly standard; however, businesses can be governed by overlapping laws, which creates duplication and confusion.[25] The process of establishment starts with the requirement to register as business entities (e.g. limited liability company, partnership or sole proprietorship). Limited liability companies first register the business name and then incorporate and register with the Office of the Administrator and Registrar General.

Major legal improvements occurred between 2008 and 2009. For example, whereas it took seven days just to do the registration with the Registrar of Companies, it now takes only two to three days (World Bank, 2009). With a total of 12 days to start a new business, Sierra Leone ranks among the top economies in West Africa. The new Companies Act[26] governs the various registration and incorporation procedures. It has considerably improved the uncoordinated way in which various agencies intervened in the business registration and licensing process in the previous outdated version of the Act. A Corporate Affairs Commission has been created with a major function —regulating and supervising the incorporation and registration of companies.

However, while the new Companies Act allows for more modern and investment-friendly treatment, there is still room for improvement. For example, there are still six steps to register a business, involving four different entities (World Bank, 2009).[27] Before a business can start operations, a mandatory general business licence must be obtained from the Office of the Administrator and Registrar General. To operate in Freetown, another licence needs to be obtained from the City Council. There are also activity-specific (construction, retail, etc.) and sector-specific (tourism, telecommunications, mining, etc.) licences. In many cases they overlap (e.g. the general business licence and the licence from the City Council) and their application criteria and administration are unclear. In many cases the licensing system seems to be used more for revenue collection rather than for concrete policy purposes. Therefore, a review of the complete licence structure is needed to ease the burden and cost for business establishment. The assessment of the system should aim at maintaining those licences that are deemed necessary notably to protect: (1) health; (2) consumers and workers; (3) environment; and (4) ensure safety. Once this exercise is completed, clear and transparent guidelines should be published on the criteria and procedures to be fulfilled to obtain licences.

Against this background, the new Companies Act reduced business registration and related procedures, and the Corporate Affairs Commission serves as the regulator for registration and companies procedures. While these initiatives constitute a real progress in the business start-up process, the Act needs to be effectively implemented to have a tangible impact on the ease of doing business. Similarly, the commission needs to have the appropriate tools and means in view of efficiently coordinating business registration. Its role could be extended to simplifying licensing requirements, computerizing procedures and providing technical training to officials. In addition, SLIEPA could play a role, if added to the SLIEPA Act, in facilitating entry and establishment of businesses. Performing this task could also serve as a way to gather relevant information about foreign investment projects.

---

[24] Other key changes regarding business registration included the elimination of the use of an attorney for the preparation of the memorandum and articles of association; annual renewal of business licences; and the payment of the advance tax.

[25] These include: the Companies Ordinance (1938); the Business Names Registration Ordinance (1954); the Business Registration Act (1983); the National Revenue Authority Act (2000); the General Law (Business Start-up) (Amendment) Act (2007); and the Registration of Business Act (2007).

[26] The new Companies Act was issued in 2009, in replacement of the 1938 version.

[27] The main entities involved include: (1) the Office of the Administrator and Registrar General; (2) the National Revenue Authority; (3) Municipalities; and (4) the Ministry of Labour and Social Security.

## 2.  Taxation

The principal taxes affecting businesses are taxes on corporate profits and dividends; sales taxes; and import and excise duties.[28] The National Revenue Authority (NRA)[29] administers taxes related to income, sales, customs, excise and mineral royalties. The NRA operates with very limited resources; for example, in 2008 it still had limited computer equipment and capacity to use it. Furthermore, the large informal sector (60 to 80 per cent of GDP) imposes significant constraints in achieving revenue collection targets.

### a.  Corporate income tax

The Income Tax Act of 2000 provides the legal basis for income taxation. Sierra Leone has traditionally applied a high rate of corporate income tax but the economic reform programme of recent years recognized the importance of putting in place a more competitive regime. A first step was made in 2005 to reduce the corporate tax rate from 35 to 30 per cent, except in mining, which remains at 35 per cent. Losses may be carried forward indefinitely but the amount that can be applied in any one year cannot reduce taxable income by more than 50 per cent.

### Table II.2. Capital allowances, loss carry-forward and general incentives

| Fiscal measures | Application |
|---|---|
| **Standard capital allowance (declining balance, per cent)** | **Depreciable assets** |
| 40 | Plant, machinery and equipment, including automobiles and trucks |
| 10 | Other tangible depreciable assets except buildings, intangible assets |
| 15 | Buildings housing industrial, manufacturing, agricultural activities |
| 10 | Buildings housing commercial activities other than the previous |
| 5 | Buildings other than those described in the previous groups |

**Loss carry-forward**

Loss carry-forward is permitted to the extent that the loss has not been deducted in a previous year of assessment insofar as the tax payable each year will be less than 50 per cent of the tax due if such loss is not carried forward.

**Other measures**

| | |
|---|---|
| Sales tax | Exemption from payment of sales tax for importation of plant, machinery and spares. |
| Income tax | • Exemption of 5 per cent of business income derived from export sales;<br>• A 100 per cent deduction for research and development costs;<br>• An investment allowance of 5 per cent (deducted from business income) of the cost of plant, machinery and equipment, including automobiles and trucks;<br>• A business investment relief deduction (maximum 50 per cent of investment totalling not more than Le 3 million ($1,000)) in any year of assessment for five years from resident individuals' income (not owners, partners, managers, employees or creditors) for purchase of up to 30 per cent of newly issued ordinary shares in a company. |

*Sources*: Income Tax Act of 2000; the Mines and Minerals Act (Decree); the Development of Tourism Act.

---

[28] Other taxes include: payroll on foreign employees; entertainment (10 per cent of ticket price); restaurant (10 per cent); tourism (7.5 per cent); 0.5 per cent charge of cost, insurance and freight (CIF) value; agricultural exports (2.5 per cent of f.o.b. value); telecommunications (10 per cent on all telephone calls); foreign travel (10 per cent). Withholding taxes cover rental, dividend, royalties and interests. The personal income tax has a progressive structure with a top marginal rate of 30 per cent applied to all income above Le 7.5 million.

[29] The NRA started in 2003 and is organized in Income Tax, Customs/Excise, Gold/Diamond and Non-Tax Revenue Units. Key laws include the Income Tax Act (2000); Customs Tariff Act (1978); Excise Act (1982); and Sales Tax Act (1995).

The standard fiscal regime provides measures such as tax depreciation allowances with a generous rate of 40 per cent for plant and machinery, competitive depreciation rates of 10 or 15 per cent on most types of buildings and other general incentives (table II.2). Moreover, the asset base is inflation indexed. Special treatment of tax depreciation is provided for mining and, to a lesser extent, for tourism to recognize the special features of investment in these industries (table II.3).

On payments to non-residents, withholding tax is imposed at a rate of 10 per cent on dividends, 15 per cent on interest and 10 per cent on services. Sierra Leone has only four DTTs, three of which are more than 50 years old. These are with the United Kingdom (1947 and 2000), Denmark (1954), Norway (1954) and India (1956). In the latest treaty with the United Kingdom, dividends and royalty payments to non-residents are tax exempt. Investors' interests in Sierra Leone would be encouraged by an expansion of DTTs, in particular with new important partners and countries with firms active in key areas of FDI (e.g. mining) such as Australia, Canada, China, France, the Gambia, Ghana, Nigeria, South Africa and Switzerland. The ECOWAS Treaty provides for the negotiation of a convention on double taxation. To date, no progress has been achieved on this important endeavour that would be useful in facilitating regional investment into Sierra Leone.

### Table II.3. Incentives and special industry regimes

| Sector | Incentives |
| --- | --- |
| Agriculture | • Ten-year exemption from income tax for rice and tree crops production (cocoa, coffee, palm oil). Dividends paid in the exemption period are free of tax for individual farmers and taxed at 50 per cent of the applicable rate for companies engaged in farming;<br>• Custom duty exemption on agriculture inputs (fertilizers, seeds, pesticides, tractors/parts, machinery). |
| Tourism | • Fifteen per cent corporate income tax, limited to a maximum of 150 per cent of eligible expenditures of the original capital invested, for the first five years of a new investment;<br>• Investment allowance of 5 per cent of the cost of the relevant asset in acquiring new assets of plant, machinery and equipment, including automobiles and trucks, and commercial buildings;<br>• Exemption from payroll taxes during three years for up to six non-citizen employees with skills not available;<br>• Duty free for new construction, extension or renovation of existing facilities, applicable to building materials, machinery or equipment that is not easily available in Sierra Leone;<br>• The Tourism Act (1990) article 37 gives discretionary powers to the Tourism Minister to grant further tax relief. |
| Mining | • Royalties of 5 per cent on precious stones, 4 per cent on precious metals and 3 per cent on other minerals;<br>• 35 per cent corporate income tax;<br>• Immediate amortization of pre-production exploration and prospecting expenditure;<br>• For mine development expenditure, tax depreciation of 40 per cent in year of expenditure; 20 per cent of cost for each of next three years (straight line basis);<br>• Write-offs against profits on funds put aside for future expenses for mine closure and rehabilitation;<br>• Importation free of customs duty, charges and levies on machinery, plant and other equipment used "exclusively for the conduct of prospecting and exploration operations";<br>• Election to have accounts denominated in United States dollars;<br>• Each project under common ownership is ring fenced for tax purposes;<br>• The fiscal terms set out in the law can form part of a mine development agreement with the government and hence be stabilized. |

*Sources*: Income Tax Act (2000, 2004 amendment); Mines and Minerals Act (Decree); the Development of Tourism Act.

The tax authority may set minimum levels of taxable income for a company – either 10 or 15 per cent of turnover, depending on whether adequate accounts are kept. This does not apply to a company that submits audited accounts. There is also a designated set of 50 small-scale business activities to which a fixed minimum tax applies.

The chargeable income of a resident taxpayer is the taxpayer's assessable income from all sources. A branch in Sierra Leone of a non-resident company is subject to income tax on chargeable income plus dividend withholding tax on the higher of funds repatriated or retained earnings.

Advance tax payments apply based on estimated turnover or taxable income for the year. Firms pay quarterly provisional taxes (25 per cent at a time) on the basis of forecasts. When estimated tax payments are higher than actual results, the difference is credited to the following year as it is difficult to obtain the refunds that the law authorizes.

Sierra Leone applies various compliance measures. For importers, there is a pre-payment of income tax of 3 per cent of the CIF price of imports (unless the taxpayer submits audited accounts). A withholding tax of 5 per cent is levied on payments to resident contractors. Thin capitalization rules apply to expensing interest costs on shareholder loans.

The Income Tax Act has provisions concerning transfer pricing based on an arm's length transaction approach; however, no regulations and guidelines have yet been produced.

Sierra Leone has specific fiscal measures (table II.3) for activities in agriculture, tourism and mining. The agriculture and tourism industry measures include corporate income tax holidays although, in tourism, the extent of the holiday is constrained by the amount invested. The mining fiscal regime was developed in the early 1990s to provide internationally competitive arrangements for that time (see section dealing with mining.)

Figure II.1 compares the tax burden in four sectors (agriculture, manufacturing, tourism and fisheries) in Sierra Leone with other developing countries.[30] The comparison is based on the tax system in place in 2008, incentives and UNCTAD's comparative tax methodology (annex 2). The discounted present value of tax is measured as a percentage of investors' cash flow (present value of tax in per cent). The higher the present value of tax (in per cent), the greater the tax burden on an investment.

The burden estimated with standard taxes in Sierra Leone is similar to that in the four sectors in the other countries. This is due to Sierra Leone's decision to reduce the corporate tax rate to 30 per cent as well as its attractive tax depreciation allowances; however, the latter is somewhat diluted by the cap on the loss carry-forward. The government should make sure to have sufficient revenues to finance public expenditures through an effective fiscal regime. While avoiding a "race to the bottom", the government could consider bringing the country in line with other regional economies, such as Côte d'Ivoire, Ghana or Mauritania (their corporate tax rate is 25 per cent).[31] To optimize the impact of this measure, it would be useful to implement it in concert with the simplification of other taxes and the introduction of facilitation services related to tax compliance. Reducing the corporate tax could also encourage firms to move to the formal sector. For this to happen, this measure should be supported by the introduction of an efficient refund mechanism of value added taxes (see section on indirect taxes, below).

---

[30] The selection of comparison countries takes into consideration regional competitors, relevant economic features and other countries that have successfully developed certain sectors and success in attracting FDI in those activities.

[31] The total short-term revenue impact of reducing corporate rates by 10 percentage points (a drop in tax revenue of about $5 million) would probably be small since corporate tax revenue ($16.5 million) represented 10 per cent of total tax revenues in 2007. In the medium and long term, the small decrease in revenue should be compensated by rises in tax revenues from both direct and indirect taxes that would result from higher investments and an increased number of firms operating in the formal sector.

**Figure II.1. Comparative taxation of investment, 2008**
(Present value of tax as a percentage of investors' cash flow)

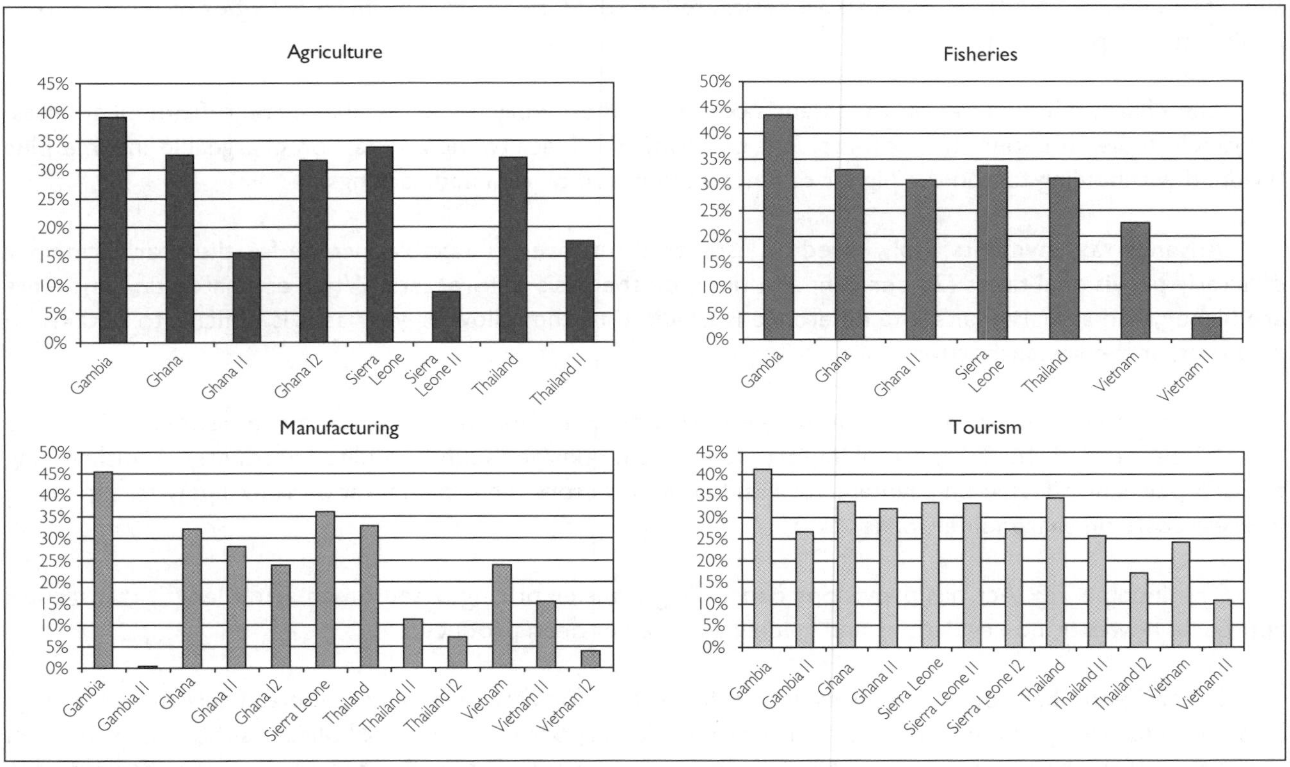

*Source*: UNCTAD.

Note: I1 and I2 refer to different investment incentives in the country used for the comparison. Annex 2 provides details about the specific programmes used in the simulation.

In agriculture, Sierra Leone maintains an incentive scheme for tree crops and rice. In fisheries, neither Sierra Leone nor the other African countries that are being compared maintain incentive schemes. Furthermore, Sierra Leone is one of few countries that does not promote investment in manufacturing through sector-specific tax incentives (e.g. export processing zones). In tourism, Sierra Leone's incentive scheme compares well with the other African comparator countries but it is not as ambitious.

The IPA of 2004 introduced the possibility of implementing an incentive scheme. The details of its structure have yet to be agreed upon. Rather than amending the Act to include a detailed incentive structure, the Government of Sierra Leone should consider using the Income Tax Act to define such a structure. For clarity, if this option was selected, the IPA should reflect the fact that fiscal incentives are dealt with in the Income Tax Act. Their implementation would then be the responsibility of the Ministry of Finance and the National Revenue Authority. This would be useful in preventing dispersion and policy inconsistency.

The definition and introduction of additional incentives (e.g. beyond the measures that are in place) should be evaluated with caution as there is evidence on the ineffectiveness of incentives to promote investment (box II.1). Against this background, improving the general tax rules and ensuring their competitiveness should remain the focus.

In 2008, the Trade Ministry developed a draft proposal for investment incentives. In agriculture, it increases the number of activities eligible for the 10-year tax holiday and provides an investment allowance

> ## Box II.1. The experience of investment incentives for the attraction of FDI
>
> International experience shows mixed outcomes with respect to the use of incentives to attract FDI. Positive experiences resulted in economies such as the Republic of Korea, Singapore and Taiwan Province of China. On the other hand, countries such as Egypt and Indonesia have, in recent years, streamlined their fiscal incentives and put in place an improved tax regime to attract investment. Furthermore, an evaluation of the numerous incentives used by South Africa pointed to the need for reform. In this regard, it is recommended to improve the tax regime rather than focusing on incentives to attract investment. Ireland is cited as a model to illustrate the role of incentives in promoting investment. It adopted a series of tax incentives in the early 1980s. It is only in the mid-1990s that major investment projects took place. Macroeconomic stability, lower tax rates, reforms of administrative procedures and European Union (EU) membership are however considered to be the main factors behind these projects.
>
> To be attractive to investors, tax systems must function well (reasonable tax rates, transparency, simplicity and stability) and be supported by sound macroeconomic conditions as well as good regulatory and institutional frameworks. The trend is therefore to lowering corporate income taxes as a means to attract FDI.
>
> However, if tax incentives are used, consideration should be given to the following issues: (i) tax incentives (accelerated depreciation and investment allowances/tax credits) used for the rapid recovery of investment costs can be more cost-effective than reducing corporate income tax rates; (ii) tax holidays of total exemption of corporate income tax are the least desirable measures; (iii) indirect tax incentives are very prone to abuse and should perhaps be limited to the removal of customs duties on inputs that are used in the direct production of exports; (iv) any tax incentive must be based on transparent legal provisions; and (v) qualifying criteria for incentives must be based on simple and objective considerations.
>
> *Sources:* OECD (2003) and Barbour (2005).

for an additional five years. It introduces the South-East Asian concept of pioneer and priority status industries that would enjoy a five-year full or partial tax holiday. It also includes additional investment allowances in a wide range of industries, including manufacturing. Given the capacity constraints of the NRA, the time to administer these fiscal incentives and the international evidence presented in box II.1, there is a need to reconsider this proposal. Typically, Asian countries apply minimum investment size eligibility thresholds to reduce administrative requirements: however, this results in discrimination against small investors.[32]

Against this background, Sierra Leone should not hesitate to improve the effectiveness and attractiveness of the fiscal regime in order to be in line with other regional economies (e.g. Côte d'Ivoire, Ghana or Mauritania). It should start with a competitive general regime followed by specific schemes targeted at sectors and results such as the agro-processing and export manufacturing. With respect to general measures, the Government of Sierra Leone should consider the following recommendations:

- Review the general rate of corporate income tax and apply it to all business, including special development operations or zones;
- Remove restrictions on the utilization of loss carry-forward;
- Reduce and harmonize to between 5 and 10 per cent all withholding taxes on payments to service contractors, royalties, interests and dividends;
- Review advance tax payments to eliminate the 3 per cent charge on CIF imports. Also limit the advance turnover tax payments for taxes that have been paid in a previous year;
- Negotiate DTTs with key partners and finalize the negotiations for an ECOWAS DTT;

---

[32] An investment promotion agency in charge of administering investment incentives can give a misleading impression of its performance in attracting investment. In that case, investors may interact with the agency because it is the incentives gateway and not necessarily because of its capacity to promote and facilitate investment. UNCTAD (2004) provides an analysis of the effects of discretionary incentives.

- Eliminate provisions on sector laws (e.g. tourism) that give discretionary power to grant investment incentives;
- Apply the same income tax rate to resident and non-resident small business owners;
- Clarify provisions concerning minimum chargeable business income tax;
- Establish a special project window to facilitate the provision of administrative services for large strategic investments.

With respect to sector-specific features, the recommendations are to:
- Provide low or zero corporate income tax on export sales by agro-processing and general manufacturing industries (income on domestic sales would be subject to the standard tax rate). For a least developed country, this is unlikely to be of concern under the WTO rules on export subsidies;
- Introduce universally available and easily administered measures to promote specific outcomes (such as additional deductions for large-scale employment) and to address difficulties (such as investment allowances for self-provision of utilities and infrastructure);
- Allow investment in selected infrastructure to qualify for tax relief on unrelated income of the investor.

### b. Indirect taxes

Sierra Leone has, at the moment, a sales tax of 15 per cent. A decision has been made to replace it with a value added tax (VAT). Care should be taken so that the VAT: is introduced at a reasonable rate; is broadly based; has an efficient reimbursement mechanism; has no or few exemptions; and applies a rate of zero on exports. The government has indicated that these elements are taken into account in the plan for the VAT.

The VAT can be an effective measure to promote investment and increase competitiveness by reducing indirect taxes on business inputs[33] and lowering the tax embedded in the prices of exports. Therefore, the implementation of this tax is a priority for the government.

### 3. Export processing zones and export promotion measures

An important constraint to diversifying and increasing exports of goods and services in Sierra Leone is the absence of a competitive production sector. This prevents the country from tapping the benefits of trade preferences, which grant the country unlimited access to important global markets. While export processing zones could be a potential solution, the country has no legal provisions in place to operate them. Furthermore, and under the current conditions, exporting from Sierra Leone is a lengthy and complicated process (WTO, 2004).

As of 2008, there was no customs duty drawback scheme in place that would, if well designed, be useful in fostering exports. A duty drawback regime for both direct and indirect exporters would allow businesses to rapidly obtain inputs at world prices. Clear guidelines, timely processing of documents and prompt payment of claims would be essential to the success of the programme. One efficient administrative option is to implement a computerized customs system to register transactions and to calculate and process the duty drawback refunds on the spot. An alternative system is to set up a fund at the Central Bank (funded by collected tariff duties) to pay for the duty drawback (e.g. Zambia's system). The introduction of a VAT system, with an efficient reimbursement mechanism, would be a very good complementary measure and a significant improvement for business operations if coordinated with an automatic duty drawback. Finally, it is also recommended to adopt additional measures to allow direct duty-free importation of selected inputs for the production of exports. The World Customs Organization Revised Kyoto Convention provides guidelines on how this can be established, including operational guidelines.

---

[33] This measure would also remove price distortions between products that use taxable inputs and those that do not.

## 4.   Customs procedures

Customs clearance and technical controls (either for importation or exportation) on average cost $550 and take six days (World Bank, 2009). The numerous and lengthy customs procedures discourage doing business in Sierra Leone. This is particularly problematic for foreign investors who depend heavily on the importation of inputs. Solving problems related to customs procedures would lower trading costs and enhance competitiveness. Ideally, this should occur in parallel with port and trade procedure improvements. Infrastructure limitations, poor law enforcement and accounting make auditing on a post-importation basis difficult; such problems need to be considered within customs reforms to provide coherence and more comprehensive measures.

The Customs Act (Cap. 271) and the Customs Tariff Act (1978) regulate the work of the Customs and Excise Department of the NRA.[34] The Department of Customs Operations is in charge of customs administration. In 2008, the NRA applied pre-shipment inspection (PSI) procedures for commercial imports of a minimum value of $2,000.[35] The documents needed to clear imports include the bill of landing, the commercial invoice, the bill of entry, the delivery order and the packing list.[36] The private firm Intertek Ltd, responsible for preparing the PSI, issues the import duty report to the importer and the NRA evaluates the customs duty by comparing the import duty report, the importer invoice and the customs valuation database, which contains the value declared by previous importers or confirmed by Intertek. The highest of the three is considered the value for duty.

Reference values (officially "established minimum customs values") are maintained for imports of sensitive items (rice, flour, sugar, cement, plastic slippers, used clothing and used clothing accessories). Publicly available information on these values is difficult to find. A clearance permit for rice, flour and sugar is granted when the payment of a 40 per cent deposit of assessed customs duties is made and a bank guarantee to secure the outstanding balance is presented. The remaining 60 per cent is to be paid in the next three months. This is an overly restrictive and expensive requirement that should be simplified.

In early 2008, Sierra Leone had not implemented the WTO Agreement on Customs Valuation, as institutional limitations made this difficult. Furthermore, the Bank of Sierra Leone determines the exchange rate that is used for customs valuation purposes. This policy needs to be aligned with article 9 of the WTO Customs Valuation Agreement, which requires that the exchange rate used for these transactions reflects, as closely as possible, the value of the currency used for commercial transactions. A new customs law is being drafted which, when completed, will consolidate the various laws currently in force. These outdated laws are not transparent, allow for little predictability and require inefficient procedures. In addition, updating these laws would permit the use of modern technologies for customs procedures.

There are a number of technical assistance initiatives to strengthen customs operations in Sierra Leone. They focus on, among other things, the setting and implementation of the Customs Department as a one-stop centre. They will also provide assistance for the implementation of an integrated computer system, with the setting up of the ASYCUDA++ system. The pilot project was launched in 2008 and its implementation is imminent. Functional training has been provided for customs officers and customs management is planned in the near future. It should considerably improve customs clearance procedures.

To address the customs procedures challenges, the Government of Sierra Leone should:
*   Put in place a new Customs Law that includes: (a) the WTO Agreement on Customs Valuation;

---

[34] Complementary laws also include the: Customs Tariff Ordinance of 1932 (as amended); Customs Ordinance 1948/49; Customs Regulation of 1948; and the Customs (Import and Export) Order in Council of 1952.

[35] With UNCTAD's automated system for customs data (ASYCUDA) which is being implemented (see below), the PSI will no longer be needed. In fact, the PSI is scheduled to be replaced by the destination inspection. This should lower import transaction costs. At present, the inspection charge payable by the importer is set at 1.1 per cent of the free on board (FOB) value. If the FOB value is lower than $20,455, importers pay a minimum charge of $225.

[36] Import duties have rates of 0, 5, 15 and 20 per cent, depending on the type of good; the import sales tax is levied at 15 per cent of the CIF value of imports; an ECOWAS levy is also charged at 0.5 per cent.

(b) the use of the Harmonized Commodity Description and Coding System (HS) of tariff nomenclature; and (c) a risk management approach for customs inspection;

- Finalize the corresponding customs regulations to operationalize the new law;
- Eliminate the use of PSI procedures, reference values, deposit payment requirements and bank guarantees for granting clearance permits;
- Effectively implement and use the ASYCUDA++ system in order to improve the processing of import and export information, customs warehouse inventory control, statistical reporting and customs declarations;
- Establish a new coordination mechanism to better connect the various agencies involved with import and export clearances;
- Introduce a modern and harmonized customs procedure to support the transit of goods from neighbouring countries;
- Establish a medium-term training programme (e.g. five years) to build technical capacity with a focus on: customs procedures; customs information systems; technical auditing; customs warehousing; effective risk management methods; and anti-smuggling procedures.

## 5.    Foreign exchange arrangements

The Bank of Sierra Leone Act (2000) defines a market-determined exchange rate system and assigns to the Central Bank regulatory and supervisory responsibilities for foreign exchange operations. For short periods, the Central Bank may restrict the purchase, sale, holding or transfer of foreign exchange in order to avert a foreign exchange crisis. In 2007, the IMF reclassified the exchange rate system as a crawling peg to reflect the recent stability of the nominal exchange rate.

Residents and non-residents are permitted to maintain foreign currency accounts denominated in any convertible currency. The accounts can be credited with funds transferred from abroad and balances on these accounts can be converted into leones. Transfers abroad from foreign currency accounts are permitted by the law for international transactions.

In 1995, Sierra Leone accepted the provisions of IMF article VIII. In 2001, Sierra Leone removed the remaining exchange restriction, a tax clearance certificate for payments and transfers of certain types of transactions. Access to foreign currency is possible according to demand and supply conditions and market interventions by the Bank of Sierra Leone. Few legal restrictions for movement of capital remain in place. For example, the Anti-Money Laundering Act (2005)[37] restricts some forms of capital inflows to protect against destabilization resulting from laundering and criminal transactions.

No requirements are in place to surrender export earnings except in the case of financing diamond operations.[38] Exporters must repatriate proceeds within 90 days of the date of export. Proceeds from exports of diamonds that were pre-financed from external sources are not subject to the repatriation requirement. In addition to the Bank of Sierra Leone Act (2000), the 2004 IPA provides rights for the repatriation of earnings and the proceeds of sales of assets and profits, and allows expatriate employees to repatriate earnings. There are no transfer restrictions for the repayments of principal and interest on foreign loans.

Despite the unrestricted approach of the Bank of Sierra Leone Act and the IPA on foreign exchange transactions, some sector laws are outdated and maintain provisions that condition or restrict the transfers of funds abroad (e.g. the Development of Tourism Act (1990), the Exchange Control Act (Cap. 265)). This can create confusion and uncertainty. In this regard, an overall revision of these laws would be required to avoid inconsistencies regarding legal rights on foreign exchange transactions.

---

[37] These restrictions relate to (i) the use of cash or bearer securities for payments exceeding 25 million leones (about $8.3 million) in business trans-actions in one day per customer by financial institutions; and (ii) the transfer to or from any country of funds exceeding $10,000 other than by or through a financial institution.

[38] In this case, exporters must ensure that the inflows of dollars are channelled through the banking system (see Bank of Sierra Leone, http://www.bankofsierraleone-centralbank.org/diamond_export_guidelines.html).

## 6. Labour regulations

The Regulations of Wages and Industrial Relations Act (1971) and the Employers and Employed Act (1960) regulate labour issues including: minimum wages; contributions; leave allowances; redundancy or dismissal procedures; compensation; breaches of contract; and disputes between employer and employee.[39] Given that 60 to 80 per cent of GDP is generated in the informal sector, most employment is informal and unregulated.

Employment is governed by collective bargaining agreements, usually negotiated every two years. Workers have the right to organize and form trade unions. Workers have the right to strike but anti-union discrimination and retaliation against strikers are not prohibited by law. Collective bargaining agreements are widespread in the formal economy and negotiations take place in trade group negotiating councils. A Bargaining Certificate is issued by the Ministry of Labour at the end of the process. It is unclear whether firms have the right to opt out of these agreements (either individually or by declining membership in a business association).

Under collective agreements, the minimum monthly wage in the formal sector was about $24 in 2007 while the statutory minimum salary was about $16 (48,000 leones). Such wage levels are among the lowest in Africa and probably globally as well (table II.4). They do not provide sufficient living standards to the workers and are symptomatic of the low level of productivity due to the lack of training and employment opportunities. Sierra Leone should thus aim at increasing training programmes for workers in order to raise labour productivity and thus salaries. It is also advisable to increase the statutory minimum wage to a decent level in order to improve living conditions.

### Table II.4. Comparative wages and labour features

| | Approximate 2007 minimum monthly wage ($) | Population (millions) | Population under age 15 (per cent) | Urban population (per cent) |
|---|---|---|---|---|
| **Sierra Leone** | **24** | **6.0** | **42.8** | **40.7** |
| Burundi | 28 | 8.0 | 45.1 | 10.0 |
| Madagascar | 35 | 19.0 | 43.8 | 26.8 |
| Guinea Bissau | 38 | 1.6 | 47.4 | 30.0 |
| Liberia | 40 | 3.4 | 47.0 | 58.1 |
| Gambia | 43 | 1.6 | 41.2 | 53.9 |
| Ghana | 45 | 22.5 | 39.0 | 47.8 |
| Senegal | 67 | 11.7 | 42.2 | 41.6 |
| Nigeria | 71 | 141.4 | 44.3 | 48.2 |
| Côte d'Ivoire | 78 | 18.6 | 41.7 | 45.0 |

Note: The precise comparison of labour costs is difficult to make mainly due to the lack of data on the different variables that compose the total labour bill. Available data on minimum wages is used as a proxy.
Sources: UNDP, Human Development Indexes. For wages, data reported by the United States Department of State, Bureau of Democracy, Human Rights, and Labour, http://www.state.gov/g/drl/rls/hrrpt/2007/100503.htm.

Other labour costs are also relatively moderate; however, the costs of hiring and firing workers tend to create risk aversion (table II.5). On a number of occasions unions have negotiated, notably in the case of redundancies, when firms could not comply with prescribed payments.

---

[39] Several other statutes contain labour provisions. These include: the Trade Unions Act (chapter 221) (consolidated to 1960); the Child Rights Act (2007); the Recruiting of Workers Ordinance (chapter 216) (consolidated to 1960); the Minimum Wage Act (1997); the Workmen's Compensation Act (chapter 219) (consolidated to 1960).

### Table II.5. Key labour provisions

| Issue | Treatment under labour legislation |
|---|---|
| Hours of work | • 40 hours per week for most workers. Hours worked in rest days are paid double time. The working hour per week and the days involved can vary by written agreements between the employer and the union. |
| Annual leave | • Varies according to years of service, between 1–3 years of service is 21 days, over 15 years of service is 38 days;<br>• Additional leave benefits include: two days travelling time each way for vacation leave and a leave allowance of Le 60,000. |
| Rent allowance | • Le 8,000 per month for all categories of workers. |
| Termination of service | Employers must give one month salary in lieu of notice except for disciplinary dismissal as follows:<br>• One to five years of continuous service: 30 days for each year;<br>• 5–10 years of service: 37 days for each year;<br>• Over 10 years: 42 days for each year. |
| Redundancy | • Before declaring any worker redundant, the employer must try to use the worker in an alternative position. The employer must give the worker's union three months' notice when declaring redundancy. Workers must be informed no less than two months in advance;<br>• Workers must be dismissed based on seniority but taking into account skill, ability and performance. Discharged workers are placed on a recall list for 20 weeks. |
| Compensation for redundancy | • One to five years of continuous service: 30 days for each year;<br>• 5–10 years of service: 35 days for each year;<br>• Over 10 years: 40 days for each year. |
| Transport allowance | • Le 30,000 per month for all workers. |
| Grievance procedure | • Grievance procedures include initial consultations for amicable settlement. In the event of unsuccessful outcome, either party can report the matter to the Commissioner of Labour. If the matter remains unsettled, either party can report it to the Minister of Labour. |

*Sources:* The Regulations of Wages and Industrial Relations Act No. 18 of 1971; Government Notice No. 74, 1 March 2002 (Terms and Conditions of Employment Agreed by the Services Trade Group Negotiating Council).

Employment contract duration can be definite or indefinite. Definite contracts are converted into indefinite contracts after two renewals of a two-year contract. Workers can be declared redundant either for commercial or financial reasons. After trying and failing to find alternative employment (based on retraining or reassignment), the employer can discharge workers but a seniority criterion is used after taking into account skill, ability and performance. The latter requirements tend to create limitations for restructuring needs and the efficient use of labour resources.

Workers can also be dismissed for reasons of incompetence, inefficiency, violation of rules or serious offences. After two written warnings, an employee can be dismissed without compensation. There is an appeal process on labour decisions via employer-union consultations. Following an unsuccessful intervention of the Commissioner of Labour, disputes are submitted to the Ministry of Labour, which tries to solve the matter through arbitration. If the dispute cannot be settled by arbitration within 21 days, it is then referred to the Industrial Court.

Sierra Leone has ratified 33 conventions of International Labour Organization (ILO), including six out of the eight core ILO conventions.[40] However, the institutional capacity to enforce these conventions is low.

In 2009, Sierra Leone ranked 166 out of 183 countries on the overall "employment index" of the World Bank Doing Business Report (World Bank, 2009). In comparison, the Gambia, Mali and Ghana rank 85, 100 and 133 respectively. While the Labour Code of Sierra Leone contains the basic provisions governing employment contracts, many of its articles need to be updated to reflect best practices in comparator or neighbouring countries. Introducing more flexibility would require reducing the cost of ending contracts or declaring workers redundant for restructuring purposes (the cost in 2009 was significantly higher that for sub-Saharan countries). On the other hand, there is a need to better protect workers' rights to strike without retaliation and anti-union discrimination. Furthermore, since different laws deal with labour issues, there is need to review them with the objective of consolidating them into a new Labour Act.

## 7.   Employment of foreigners

The Sierra Leonean labour market is characterized by an acute shortage of skilled workers and professionals. This situation is a serious constraint for foreign companies that constantly seek to fill managerial and technical positions. This impedes progress in diversifying the economy and attracting FDI beyond the mining sector. The law requires foreign investors to apply for a self-employment permit and foreign employees for a work permit. However, reactive immigration policies with long and costly procedures to obtain the permits exacerbate the problems.

Separate acts and ministries govern the issuance of work and residence permits for foreigners in Sierra Leone.[41] The country utilizes labour market tests but does not impose training or localization requirements to grant work permits in accordance with the General Law (Business Start-up Act, amendment) of 2007. Although this Act amended previous legislation to simplify procedures, it maintains a restrictive approach. For example, it requires that applications be submitted six months in advance to the Work Permit Committee. In making recommendations, the committee considers, among other factors, whether: (i) Sierra Leonean workers are available; (ii) granting the permit will adversely affect the wages and working conditions of Sierra Leoneans; (iii) the applicant has laid off employees in the last three months; and (iv) operations will be substantially disrupted without the targeted foreign worker. The minister approves the issuance of work permit. The criteria used to assess applications leave room for interpretation and therefore may lead to discretionary decisions.

Other complications relate to the functioning of the Work Permit Committee. Its number of members and composition (eight high-level government officials) require bureaucratic procedures, which makes it less operational to meet the needs of investors.[42] Once granted, the permit entitles the employee to work in Sierra Leone for a period of three years. The permit may then be renewed annually.

In spite of the enactment of the new law in 2007, further changes are required. For instance, some provisions regarding the employment of foreign workers remain in older laws. Furthermore, information is not easily obtained on these important matters. To address the problems associated with the work and

---

[40] Collective Bargaining; Freedom of Association; Equal Remuneration; Discrimination; Forced Labour; Abolition of Forced Labour. Sierra Leone has not ratified the ILO core Conventions on the Worst Forms of Child Labour and on Minimum Age.

[41] The relevant laws include: the Non-Citizens (Registration, Immigration and Expulsion) Act (1965); the Nationality Act (1965); the Non-Citizen and Work Permit Act; the General Law (Business Start-up) (Amendment) Act (2007). The work permit is administered by the Ministry of Employment (Labour) and Social Security (hereinafter Ministry of Labour); the residency permit is issued by the Ministry of Internal Affairs, Local Government and Rural Development.

[42] The Committee is formed by the: Deputy Secretary of the Ministry of Labour; Chief Immigration Officer; Deputy Secretary of the Trade Ministry; Deputy Secretary of the Ministry of Development and Economic Planning; a representative from each of the following: Employers Federation, Sierra Leone Chamber of Commerce and Industry and Sierra Leone Labour Congress; and a representative of the Sierra Leone Association of NGOs (with no voting right).

residence permits for foreigners, it is recommended to:
- Adopt streamlined criteria for the issuance of work permits;
- Automatically issue a residence permit to a holder of work permit;
- Establish criteria to issue a work permit to dependents of foreign workers;
- Designate a centralized and unique unit to collect applications, approve and issue permits;
- Reform the Work Permit Committee so that it operates at the technical level rather than at the senior level;
- Eliminate the requirement that applications be submitted six months in advance and limit processing time to a maximum of one month;
- Introduce a derogation for labour market test requirements for large strategic investment projects. For example, this could be applied to sectors highlighted as priorities;
- Produce and publish guidelines on the procedures for work and residency permits.

## 8. Land

Sierra Leone has a complex dual system of land tenure that imposes restrictions on land-related investment. The government recognizes that land tenure constitutes a problem and is committed to reforms to improve investment opportunities. The main problems related to land, as acknowledged by the 2005 National Land Policy, include: outdated laws; poor functioning of land markets; indeterminate boundaries; illegal acquisition of state lands; absence of a land titling system to validate property rights; difficulty accessing land for development purposes; unclear criteria to access land; weak land administration and management systems; disputes; and poor coordination. Because it is difficult to verify ownership, land is often sold or leased illegally, thus restricting and complicating investment.

Land ownership is organized as a freehold system in Freetown and the Western Area (colonial land) while the remaining provinces are subject to a leasehold system (customary land). Different laws apply to each system and there is no unified administrative land system for the country. Sierra Leonean citizens are allowed to privately own land while foreigners can only lease it under both systems.

The main responsibility for the management of land falls under the Ministry of Lands, Country Planning and the Environment (hereinafter the Ministry of Lands).[43]

In the Western Area and Freetown, land is vested in the state, which issues freehold titles to individuals. Access can be negotiated through a grant or as a claim based on occupation criteria (adverse possession). The State Land Committee under the Ministry of Lands grants state lands through a bureaucratic process that typically takes 65 to 70 business days. Foreigners (individuals and firms) are allowed to acquire land through leases of a maximum of 21 years as stipulated by the Non-Citizens (Interest-in-Land) Act.[44] However, state land must first be leased by a Sierra Leonean before a lease transfer can be negotiated with a foreigner.

Under the freehold system, an investor can lease land by completing the following steps: (1) obtaining a licence from the Ministerial Board that authorizes the granting of land rights;[45] (2) identifying the land; (3) submitting a request to the State Land Committee for publication in the gazette; and (4) paying the first year's lease (intent). Freehold rights are registered as a separate procedure under the Registration of Instrument Act.

The freehold system can, in principle, give fairly straightforward access to land. However, there are problems related to the limited capacity of institutions to register property rights and ensure their

---

[43] The Ministry of Lands manages all land. The ministry's survey duties include the resurvey of chiefdom leases, preparation of new lease agreements and implementation of land management and information systems.

[44] In practice, leases can go up to 99 years.

[45] The board has representation from the Ministries of Trade, Lands, Finance, Development and the Attorney General.

recognition. Land is also not adequately surveyed. In addition, to better fit the needs of Sierra Leone today and attract FDI, there is a need to update the legal framework, for example the Non-Citizens Act, which was adopted in 1966.

The Provinces Land Act of 1961 governs the leasehold system in the provinces and is based on the Protectorate Ordinance (1927) and the Tribal Authorities Ordinance (1938), which vested all land in the Chiefdom Council that holds land for and on behalf of the native community. Land belongs to the descendants of original settlers or hosts of a village and is controlled by families, villages, townships, clans or chiefdoms. Each member of the family is entitled to a piece of land to farm.

Non-natives who wish to acquire land face numerous, unclear and frequently changing requirements. The known steps start with obtaining the assent of the Chiefdom Council. The person then has to get approval of the District Officer for leases that can be up to 99 years. Deeds need to be registered in Freetown in the Register General (Land Leases). A lease can be assigned by the original tenant to a second tenant providing approval of the Chiefdom Council. The costs in terms of time and money to formalize such transactions with the government are, in many cases, considered too high. As a result, many transactions are not officially recorded.

In general, under unwritten customary traditions and laws, women have very limited property rights, including to land. The practice varies however in different areas of Sierra Leone.[46] Given the important role women play in agriculture (more details in chapter III) and the fact that the government is putting emphasis on the need to develop this sector, including through FDI, there is a need to improve access of women to land both in the law and in practice. This should be taken into account in the current initiative to reform land tenure.

The fact that it is not easy to prove ownership makes it difficult for commercial banks to accept title deeds of land in the provinces as collateral. This has also discouraged potential foreign investors from developing land for more productive agriculture.

The legal framework for land is under review but progress is slow. A Land Commission Act and a Commercial Use of Land Act are being drafted. The objective of the Commercial Use of Land Act is to facilitate leasing with the option of renewal under the customary system. The Land Commission Act will establish a Land Commission[47] to govern land tenure rights. The commission will be composed of a chairperson and six members appointed by the President with approval from Parliament. While a good step forward, more comprehensive reforms will be required, in the longer term, to comprehensively address the challenges of land tenure.

Taking into account capacity constraints, there are however a number of measures that could be taken in the short term. These include the need to create better conditions for market transactions through clearer public management, organizational and administrative responsibilities. The creation of a new, perhaps independent, cadastral institution is required. Such an institution should provide direct linkages with financial institutions to secure market transactions. Adopting legal provisions for the registration of titles is a good first step to codify the new legal framework for property rights. In addition, it is also recommended to implement the proposals forwarded by the Law Reform Commission. These include: amending the Registration of Instruments Act and the Survey Act to improve registration of titles; carrying out a cadastral survey to identify each parcel; and preparing legal instruments to facilitate equity mortgage operations.

---

[46] In some areas (e.g. the east and south) women tend to enjoy greater rights, can inherit land and property and become paramount chiefs. In the north of the country, this is not the case and women have fewer rights than men. In some cases, women cannot rent houses in urban areas. Depending on the area of the country, widows can be relieved of land and property and must either return to their parents' house, or leave to find another husband (Unruh and Turray, 2006).

[47] The proposal was made by the Law Reform Commission and the Ministry of Lands. It was presented to Parliament but has yet to be approved.

Finally, another important area for progress is improving transparency. An area of action is the drafting of clear and complete procedures for access to land under the freehold and customary systems, including guidelines and information centres in Freetown and key locations in the provinces.

## 9.  Environment

Sierra Leone's key environmental provisions are contained in the National Policy on the Environment (1995) and the Environment Protection Act (2000). In addition, environmental issues are dealt with in sector laws (forestry, wildlife, minerals, fisheries, etc). The legal framework is based on the principle of "the polluter pays". There are no excessive environmental requirements imposed by these laws on business practices over and beyond standard environmental considerations.

Internationally banned chemicals are prohibited in Sierra Leone as well as the discharge of any hazardous substances into the air, land and water. The country is a party to the Convention on International Trade in Endangered Species of Wild Fauna and Flora. Sierra Leone has ratified conventions on climate change and biodiversity.

The Ministry of Lands, through its Environment Protection Division, has the responsibility for environmental issues. More specifically, the ministry is mandated to regulate standards pertaining to the use of natural resources including air and water quality, waste and noise control. The National Commission on Environment and Forestry, created in 2005, has responsibility for coordinating and managing environmental and forestry issues. However, no progress has been made to provide institutional and working capacity to this entity. The Environmental Protection Act of 2000 established the National Environment Protection Board to coordinate, set policies, review environmental impact assessments and investigate environmental issues, among other tasks.

Part II of the Environment Protection Act (2000) makes provision for environmental impact assessments (EIAs). Schedule I lists a set of projects requiring EIA licences including: farming and fisheries; hydroelectric resources; infrastructure; industrial activities; extractive industries; waste management and disposal; housing construction; and activities creating substantial changes in natural resources. Applications for EIA licences are submitted to the Director of the Environment Protection Division. Within 14 days of receiving an application, the director has to make a decision on whether an EIA is required. If an EIA is not required, the director can immediately issue the corresponding licence. In practice, EIAs are rarely undertaken.

## 10.  Governance issues

The fight against corruption is widely recognized as a key challenge to the successful consolidation of peace and the creation of favourable conditions for economic development and attraction of higher levels of FDI in Sierra Leone. The corruption perception index of Transparency International ranked Sierra Leone 150 out of 180 countries in 2007 (Thomson, 2007).

Important progress towards good governance has been achieved since the end of the war. This includes: re-establishing government authority throughout the country; reforming the armed forces and police; appointing an independent Anti-Corruption Commissioner; improving economic management including through reformed regulation of sectors (e.g. mining); establishing greater local governance capacity by setting up district councils, although rivalry with the chiefdoms persists; and approving a revised Anti-Corruption Act in 2008.

Significant challenges remain, however. They are related to the government's capacity to reform the judicial system and civil service and to tackle widespread corruption through the judicial process. During the period 2002 to 2007, the Anti-Corruption Commission investigated 60 cases, the majority of which were related to the misappropriation of public funds or properties.

First adopted in 2000, the Anti-Corruption Act was an important step to improving governance. The Act did not however go far enough to meet the more ambitious clauses of new international treaties adopted by Sierra Leone following the end of the war.[48] In addition, the Act did not provide the Anti-Corruption Commission with prosecution powers. Consequently, a new Anti-Corruption Act was adopted in 2008 to correct these problems.

The objectives of the changes introduced to the Act in 2008 are to: define offences of corrupt acquisition of wealth and the possession of unexplained wealth; provide investigation and prosecution powers to the Anti-Corruption Commission; and cooperate with foreign states in the investigation or prosecution of corrupt practices. It also includes the power to extradite foreigners who come into Sierra Leone having committed crimes in other countries.

The Act of 2008 has kept the definition of "impeding investment" as an offence by a public official whereby an investor or potential investor is coerced, compelled or induced to abandon his investment or is prevented from proceeding with his initial investment. Another key feature of the Act requires that all public officials declare their assets.

The general penalties are defined in article 130. In case of non-compliance with any requirement of the Act, a fine of no less than five million leones (about $1,700) is imposed. Any person who commits an offence is liable on conviction to a fine of no less than 30 million leones (about $10,000) or to imprisonment for three years.

Governance at local levels is also a challenge. Existing legislation (the Local Government Act of 2004) is not clear about the relationship between chiefs and councils and it has been reported that most local governments (District Councils, Chiefdom Administrations) continue to be characterized by widespread corruption.

While the 2008 Anti-Corruption Act is comprehensive, the key challenges for its effective implementation are related to the lack of financial, technical and human resources and to the poorly functioning judicial system.

The precarious situation of the judicial system not only jeopardizes the implementation of the Anti-Corruption Act but also the overall government efforts to tackle economic and social problems throughout the country (Government of Sierra Leone, 2007). The key problems include: lack of technical capacity and motivation due to low wages; very high backlogs of pending cases; lack of information and case tracking; high prevalence of corruption; few and expensive private lawyers available; prohibition to use legal assistance and representation from paralegals; no provision for pro bono services; no public defence; and very limited operational resources (computers, etc).

The establishment of a Commercial Court or tribunals to hear commercial disputes is a priority in judicial reform. The first step was taken in 2007 by setting up a division of the High Court for commercial disputes. Regional experience (e.g. Ghana, Uganda and the United Republic of Tanzania) suggests that commercial disputes are best handled in a separate, specialized court with dedicated, commercially trained judges. The Commercial Court system is expected to be established by 2010. To further strengthen the system, another useful measure is the adoption of a bankruptcy law.[49] Appropriate and specialized training for commercial judges is advisable.

---

[48] Sierra Leone is party to: the African Union Convention on Preventing and Combating Corruption (signed December 2003, not yet ratified); the United Nations Convention against Corruption (signed December 2003, ratified September 2004); and the United Nations Convention against Transnational Organized Crime (signed November 2001, not yet ratified).

[49] The commercial division at the High Court in Ghana is a good example. It has the following characteristics: no territorial restriction of jurisdiction; expeditious proceedings; strict deadlines for trial; daily hearings; short adjournments; mandatory pre-trial meetings; and mediation by judges.

## 11.  Protection of intellectual property

Sierra Leone is a member of the World Intellectual Property Organization and of the African Regional Industrial Property Organization (ARIPO).[50] As a WTO member, Sierra Leone subscribes to the Agreement on Trade-Related Intellectual Property Rights (TRIPS).[51]

The country's existing intellectual property laws deal with matters such as patents, trademarks, industrial designs and copyright and related rights. These laws were drafted and approved in the context of British rule since the beginning of the twentieth century. Most of them have not been updated to account for subsequent international treaties and modern practices.

The pre-independence Copyright Act of 1965 provides 50-year post mortem copyrights for written material, sound recordings, cinematographic films and broadcasts. However, no provision to enforce or protect reproduction rights is specified.

Since 1997, Sierra Leone has been a party to the Paris Union (Paris Convention for the Protection of Industrial Property) and the Patent Cooperation Treaty (PCT). However, no national law is in place to recognize or allow for the filing of PCT applications. The types of patent applications that are available include the re-registration of granted United Kingdom patents; national phase PCT application; ARIPO application;[52] and the ARIPO regional phase PCT application. If ARIPO requirements are met, a presumption of patent validity is made in territories designated by the applicant. However, patent protection does not cover agricultural or pharmaceutical products.

Under the Trade Marks Act, trade marks may be registered at the Register Office in Freetown. Protection is provided for 14 years with the possibility of an additional 14 years. The protection covers a word or device, and a stereotype block of the trademark. The Banjul Protocol defines a trade mark filing system that allows a single filing application either in one of contracting states or directly with ARIPO. Since Sierra Leone is a signatory of the Madrid Agreement regarding the international registration of marks, questions of consistency between the Madrid Agreement and the Banjul Protocol have been raised.

In addition to the intellectual property issues discussed above, there are a number of emerging ones of interest to Sierra Leone. These include plant variety protection, traditional knowledge, geographical indications and access to genetic resources for benefit sharing under the Convention on Biological Diversity.

At the moment, only minimum institutional capacity exists to deal with intellectual property issues including industrial property matters, through the Office Administrator and Registrar General's Department of the Ministry of Justice, and copyright and related rights, through the Sierra Leone Intellectual Property Organization (Ministry of Culture and Tourism). There is also broad consensus on the need to establish a small Sierra Leone Intellectual Property Office that would operate as an autonomous government agency to administer the intellectual property legislative framework and policy. There are proposals to establish an independent industrial property tribunal or create a specialized intellectual property division within the High Court to resolve disputes concerning patents, industrial designs and trademarks.

The country's priority needs for technical and financial cooperation in intellectual property include the need for professional legislative drafting support in priority areas. Over the short term, these are

---

[50]  Sierra Leone is dependent on ARIPO to deal with patents, trade marks, industrial designs and copyrights.

[51]  Least developed country WTO members were not required to apply the provisions of the TRIPS Agreement until 2005. This flexibility was extended until 1 July 2013 to provide protection for trade marks, copyrights, patents and other intellectual property rights. In addition, these countries will not be obliged to implement certain provisions related to pharmaceutical products until 1 January 2016.

[52]  Sierra Leone is party (without ratification) to the Harare Protocol, which requires examination of patentability by ARIPO.

updating patent, industrial design, trademark and copyright legislation, and developing a national legislation utilizing TRIPS flexibilities and safeguards, such as those needed to address access to medicines. In the longer term, specialized technical support will be needed to further reform the intellectual property regulatory framework. In the context of pressing needs to reform the judicial system and public entities in Sierra Leone, intellectual property laws and enforcement of intellectual property rights should be kept on the reform agenda. To help it deal with some of these intellectual property issues, Sierra Leone communicated to the WTO TRIPS Council these needs (WTO, 2007). This will help Sierra Leone generate support for implementing the TRIPS Agreement through multilateral and bilateral technical assistance programmes that give priority to LDCs.

## 12.  Competition law and policy

Sierra Leone has neither a competition law nor a policy in place to address competition issues. Consideration is being given to developing a competition law and a legal policy framework but no concrete action has been taken on this issue yet.

Within the existing setting of a rather basic economic structure, retail markets are dominated by small-scale enterprises and individual sellers who mainly supply basic goods and services. Manufacturing and other activities remain limited. High set-up costs and limited infrastructure impede the entry of more players into the market who could play an active role in fostering more competition. The prices of goods and services are set freely by market forces, except for the price of petroleum, which is regulated by the government.

The large number of informal enterprises raises some competition policy challenges. In sectors where informality prevails, implementing a competition law might not yield the desired results. A major challenge will be to implement competition rules in such a way that they are applicable to the majority of (if not all) economic actors in the economy.

Sierra Leone faces the typical tension confronting many small economies between highly concentrated industries, characterized by a small number of competing large firms, and a multitude of small firms that struggle to reach minimum levels of efficiency. This dichotomy constitutes a key consideration in the formulation and enforcement of an effective competition law and policy. A cautious approach should seek to prevent undue levels of concentration by prohibiting anticompetitive mergers and acquisitions for the sake of preserving competition, while taking into account the economic necessity of firms seeking to increase efficiency and derive economies of scale and scope through concentration. In this context, neither an inflexible approach to the application of merger policy nor an overly permissive approach that allows firms to unduly acquire market power (Gal, 2003) is desirable. Striving for an appropriate balance between efficiency and competitive considerations remains a key concern for any competition framework.

The priority considerations identified in this report that will need to be addressed by Sierra Leone's competition law and policy framework include: (i) pricing practices by future private operators of port services; (ii) ensuring that economic regulation by port regulatory authorities is not inimical to competition, including deciding the scope and application of competition rules to regulated sectors; and (iii) assuring that access to essential facilities is given by infrastructure owners to other service providers (e.g. access to transport facilities (roads and railways) that have been built by private companies, such as mining firms).

The UNCTAD Model Law (UNCTAD, 2007b) could serve as a basis for the formulation of the general substantive elements of the national competition law. Such elements relate to abuse of dominant market position and the relationship between the competition authority and regulatory bodies, including sectoral regulators, intellectual property and consumer protection bodies.

## 13. Selected sector issues and regulations

### a. Electricity

Despite the country's important energy potential,[53] electricity generation is still very low and insufficient to match current and potential future demand. There were small increases in 2007 and 2008 but the limited supply continues to constrain investment. In this context, the importance of electricity cannot be overstated and reforming the sector is a priority.

The electricity sector operates under the National Power Authority (NPA) Act (no. 3 of 1982), which grants to the NPA the sole responsibility for carrying out power generation, transmission and distribution. The NPA has many management and technical problems. Not least of these is that it has consistently operated at a loss due to a practice of keeping tariffs more than 20 per cent below production costs (Ministry of Energy and Power, 2007).

There are ambitious medium-term goals for 2010–2015. These include developing independent hydroelectric power projects and introducing private sector operators in distribution and supply, possibly through the creation of regional distribution companies. In addition, another ambitious goal is to interconnect the electricity grid with neighbouring countries (West African Power Pool). The sector regulatory reform and the rehabilitation of the NPA are necessary for these projects to unfold. However, this is likely to be a lengthy process.

In 2006, the NPA Act was amended to enable a new special purpose company, under government ownership. The objective was to develop the Bumbuna hydroelectric generation project. The first phase of this project would generate 50 MW, which would significantly increase generation capacity. Construction is underway but its relationship with the NPA has not been settled.

A top priority should be to put the NPA on a proper commercial footing. As a small company carrying many risks, the NPA is unable to attract sizeable private foreign investors. Instead, the best approach would be an initial rehabilitation stage under a management contract. This should be undertaken with a longer-term view towards adding generation capacity by contracting supply from independent power projects. This is consistent with current plans that envisage a two-stage process of: (1) keeping the NPA vertically integrated, with private generators entering the market and an independent regulatory agency formed; and (2) restructuring the NPA as a limited liability company. The future role of the NPA as a private firm is to be defined in the long term. The World Bank is considering assisting along these lines through a comprehensive power/water project.

A key recommended action is to have a strong technical task force supported by senior political leadership. The task force will be in charge of the implementation of the power sector reform strategy and action plan. It will also be responsible, in the short term, for improving the managerial, technical and financial capacity of the NPA. The work of the task force should include, as a priority, the definition of the characteristics of operation of the special purpose company, including its relationship with the NPA, price determination and selling arrangements.

### b. Transport

In Sierra Leone, the laws concerning transport activities are outdated and lack specific consideration for private investments in transport infrastructure. A modern and efficient regulatory framework is therefore needed. This is particularly the case given the poor status of infrastructure in the country and the need to attract FDI to develop it as recognized by the government and recent announcements by foreign investors.

---

[53] Over 21 sites for hydroelectricity have been identified with a conservative estimate of about 1,200 MW. Renewable resources include biomass, solar, wind and fossil fuels including coal and petroleum. Exploration activities have started for petroleum.

An example is the $300 million African Minerals project to rehabilitate the Pepel to Marampa railway, build an extension of the Marampa railway to Tonkolili and rehabilitate the Pepel port. This investment was triggered by the discovery of a world-class iron ore deposit in the area. It is an important project for Sierra Leone's infrastructure development. To reap its full benefits in terms of economic and social development, some challenges will have to be overcome.

From a regulatory standpoint, the framework is missing to deal with investment in the transport initiatives that are taking place. From the perspective of best international standards, entering such projects require laws and regulations that provide clear and stable bases to govern partnership agreements, an open bidding process, the inclusion of civil society and independent regulators to monitor the project. In addition, where there are laws, they tend to conflict with private investment initiatives in transport. For example, foreign firms are not permitted to engage in cargo clearing or forwarding. Private investors, foreign or domestic, cannot participate in maritime port activities as the Sierra Leone Port Authority has exclusive rights for port services. In addition, restrictions exist (partnership requirements) for investment in internal waterway transport and rail transport services. Furthermore, countries in the region receive preferential treatment for road transport (passenger and freight). These measures are inconsistent with the operational needs of firms, including those of African Minerals for the transportation and export of its iron ore.

Other issues pertaining to this project that could arise and should be planned for include contractual obligations such as building standards, maintenance, environmental impact, safety standards, land access or right-of-way and terms of use for the investor and other interested parties. There have been similar projects implemented in other countries that could be used as case studies. One example is the Guinean TransGuinea railway and deep-water port. In this instance, the country enacted a "build operate and transfer" (BOT) law and negotiated a BOT agreement that included mining concessions for the mining company developing the infrastructure. Senegal also enacted a BOT law in 2004 that encompasses all types of private-public partnerships (PPPs) and was able to successfully build the Transrail Regional Railroad System through a PPP. This does not mean that a BOT is necessarily the preferable option. Sierra Leone might also want to consider a joint venture with African Minerals or any other foreign investors interested in developing infrastructure. This type of agreement could provide the government with the ability to accommodate passenger traffic or to allow other firms access. Against this background, the Government of Sierra Leone must carefully analyse the options while keeping in mind future opportunities regarding the use of the railway and port as well as any other infrastructure built by private investors.

The Sierra Leone Maritime Administration (SLMA) Act (2000) is central to the development of maritime transport such as through the Pepel or Freetown ports. The Act created the SLMA to oversee regulatory issues, infrastructure development and freight rate administration. The SLMA Act is modern and opens the possibility for maritime transport development by public or private stakeholders. The provisions of the Act contain sufficient flexibility to accommodate future opportunities in maritime port activities, including multifunctional approaches to port services. However, the privatization of the Sierra Leone Port Authority (SLPA) services present many challenges and at present, there is no clear strategy on how to move forward, including through a landlord system. Furthermore, even though the SLMA was created in 2001, it is unclear how it will be able to oversee the regulatory duties regarding port services. In this regard, the planned overall changes for the sector provide an opportunity for institutional reorganization and sector regulation.

There are a few other additional issues in port services that require attention to move reforms forward in a more coherent manner. The Sierra Leone National Shipping Company (SLNSC) is a public firm (cargo clearing and freight forwarding services) listed for privatization. However, as mentioned above, foreign investors are prohibited from carrying out clearing and freight forwarding activities. This measure affects the capacity to privatize the SLNSC. Given the limited domestic capital and expertise available and interested in SLNSC activities, the repeal of this provision could be pursued to improve the prospects for both the privatization of the SLNSC and for FDI attraction in port services.

Another area of importance is the rehabilitation of the Freetown Airport. There are two initiatives that would allow concessions to the private sector. The first one is the privatization of the airport ground handling services that are legally owned by the Sierra National Airlines (SNA) but operated by the Sierra Leone Airport Authority since June 2006 due to the bankrupt status of the SNA. The second initiative is the takeover of the SNA.

In this context, a comprehensive revision of existing laws and the proposal of new ones are critically needed to bring coherence and consistency. This is necessary to create a conducive environment for foreign investors to participate in the development of the transport sector.

## c.  Mining

Sierra Leone's mineral endowments represent an important potential source of growth, employment, tax revenue, infrastructure and skills development (chapter I). Since the end of the war, mining activity has been recovering, but has yet to reach its pre-war levels except for gold and diamonds. Mining activities are organized as (i) large-scale production of non-precious minerals (rutile and bauxite); (ii) large-scale production of precious stones (diamonds); and (iii) artisanal and small-scale production of precious stones and minerals (diamonds and, to a lesser extent, gold). In diamonds, artisanal mining has played an important role but FDI will be critical in reactivating and developing the sector.

The current framework is legislated through the 1996 Mines and Minerals Act (which is in the process of being reviewed) and its related laws.[54] The basic rights of operation are defined in part VII of the Act, which grants exclusive or non-exclusive prospective licences, exclusive exploration licences and mining leases.

The law allows exclusive prospecting licences for up to two years, renewable twice for one year each. Non-exclusive prospecting licences can be granted for one year and are renewable for one year.

An exploration licence confers exclusive rights on the holder. Exploration licences are granted for three years and only two applications for renewals can be presented for two years each. Fifty per cent of the exploration area must be relinquished at each renewal. Transfer of exploration licences is permitted.

All prospecting and exploration licences carry requirements to undertake work programmes and to keep records of activities and results. Exploration licences have more detailed work programmes and reporting requirements. These requirements, and the relinquishment and renewal regimes, are important in ensuring that adequate work is being performed. They are designed to prevent "squatting" on potentially valuable mineralized areas and also to ensure that information on mineralization flows back to the geological survey. Some doubts have been raised (which could not be verified by this review) as to whether there is adequate setting and monitoring of work programme commitments. It is probable that information yielded by exploration and prospecting operations is not being effectively collated to update the geological survey.

Legal security is well defined for the transition from exploration to mining licences. If an application is duly made by the holder of an exploration licence, the law grants the holder the right to receive a mining lease of up to 25 years (renewable). The lack of institutional capacity has affected legal certainty on these matters.

The application for a mining lease needs to be accompanied by a feasibility study dealing with some or all of the following: mine and processing plans; plant site and facilities analysis; environmental impact assessment

---

[54] Other sector laws include amendments to the 1994 Act (1998, 2004) and the Diamond Cutting and Polishing Act (2007). The Ministry of Mineral Resources is responsible for the sector. Donor projects are in place to strengthen its capacity.

and action plan;[55] mine reclamation and rehabilitation plan; marketing and sales plan; financial analysis; capital and operating cost analysis; employment and training analysis; and proposals for procurement of goods and services obtainable in the country.

The minister grants the mining lease provided the above proposals are satisfactory. The Act contains more detailed provisions on a number of areas such as employment, sales arrangements, environment and payment of royalty. The rights and obligations of the parties can be set out in an investor-state agreement, the terms of which must be consistent with the Mines and Minerals Act. The Act contains important financial provisions to facilitate investment. These include the right to maintain accounts and pay taxes in dollars and the right to hold export proceeds in foreign currency accounts. In practice, an agreement can also include the right to settle a dispute through international arbitration.

The taxation of mining is dealt with in both the Income Tax Act (2000) and the Mines and Minerals Act. The corporate income tax rate is 35 per cent and withholding taxes are 15 per cent on interest, 10 per cent on dividends and 10 per cent on payments to non-resident service contractors. Royalty rates[56] are 5 per cent for precious stones, 4 per cent for precious metals, 0 per cent for building and industrial minerals (lime, gravel) and 3 per cent on other minerals. Various other levies apply for administrative costs and local development funds.[57] The total of these various taxes can exceed 2 per cent of product value which, in addition to royalty, is possibly too high as charges on revenue rather than income.

Allowable expenses and depreciation allowances for large-scale mining are tailored to the sector. Pre-development prospecting and exploration costs can be immediately and fully depreciated. Further exploration on the mining lease is immediately expensed. Mine development obtains a 40 per cent immediate allowance and then 20 per cent over the next 3 years. Provisions are set out to protect government revenue including market pricing of sales, the ring fencing of each lease for tax purposes,[58] thin capitalization restrictions and a cap on allowable head office expenses.

Perceptions of appropriate taxation of minerals vary with trends and cycles in minerals prices. However, it is probable that the current corporate tax burden (including the rate and base of corporate income tax plus withholdings) needs to be reduced for Sierra Leone to offer more competitive conditions. Unfortunately, it appears that investors have struck individual deals that have gone too far in reducing the government's fiscal take. It is not at all clear how this can be lawfully done without specific legislation. The Sierra Rutile Agreement, which created a specific tax regime for that investment, was indeed the subject of special legislation in 2002. However, it is reported that new tax measures have been granted without recourse to amending legislation. The details of special deals[59] (which have not been made public and were not verified for this report) are reported to include long-term tax holidays and vastly reduced royalty payments. If so, this is unnecessary to attract investment and is an inexcusable loss of badly needed government revenue.

The government has already identified the restructuring of the minerals sector as a priority and, in 2008, a new law for mining was under preparation. However, the current legal regime is serviceable and more attention is needed to setting and enforcing work programmes and relinquishment provisions. The much more urgent task is to review the fiscal terms of current mining leases and to update the current

---

[55] Part XII of the Mines and Minerals Act deals with the protection of the environment. An EIA is required as condition for granting a mining lease except in the case of leases for building and industrial minerals. There are other requirements related to the prevention, limitation or treatment of pollution. However, enforcement is very low.

[56] Royalty charges are treated as operating costs and are deductible expenses.

[57] For diamonds, a total 3 per cent export tax is charged (Consolidated Revenue 0.75 per cent, GGDO Operation Costs 0.75 per cent, Mining Community Development Fund 0.75 per cent, Independent Valuer Fees 0.40 per cent and Mines Monitoring Fees 0.35 per cent).

[58] This prevents an owner from writing off exploration and prospecting expenses of other mineral rights against profits of a mining lease.

[59] It has been reported that Sierra Rutile enjoys until 2014 a corporate and withholding tax holiday, a 1 per cent tax on fuel and a royalty of 0.5 per cent. The cumulative revenue losses of these incentives have been estimated at $98 million between 2004 and 2016. Koidu Holdings, a kimberlite diamond mining company with the largest investment, appears to also have special incentives including a tax holiday up to 2012.

standard fiscal regime. Furthermore, the new regulation could include several measures to better protect the workers and the environment in order for the population to fully benefit from the mining projects. Improved institutional capacity and effective management of the sector will help and, given the fees charged for administrative costs, it should be possible to achieve this, including with help from donors.

Additional pending issues in the mining sector include the privatization of the public firm Mining and General Services Limited (MAGS).[60] This firm provides support services to the mining sector including acting as a shipping agent and providing clearing, forwarding and travel services. The National Commission for Privatization has listed the MAGS for divestiture; however, previous legal matters are preventing the privatization from moving forward.

## 14. Assessment and recommendations

Sierra Leone has embarked upon an important reform process that has the potential to transform the investment climate and contribute to its economic and social development. This process includes a comprehensive review of the existing laws and regulations to modernize and harmonize them. The exercise also highlights areas where new laws are needed to meet the development objectives of the country.

The 2004 Investment Promotion Act, inspired by best international practices, provides an enabling framework for FDI with an open approach and no sector restrictions. However, while de facto national treatment to FDI is granted, it is desirable to formalize it in the law. With respect to sectoral laws, a few restrictions remain, mainly in services activities. Reforming these laws to ensure a fully open investment regime should therefore be considered.

In addition to these measures and on the basis of the analysis of this chapter, six strategic areas of action are highlighted to improve the regulatory framework for FDI. These are:

### a. Establishing a competitive and effective fiscal regime

An attractive fiscal regime is an essential element to stimulate investment and ensure adequate revenue streams to finance public expenditures. Sierra Leone should thus strive to collect the necessary revenues through an effective fiscal regime. However, since the government has put FDI promotion at the centre of its development strategy, the fiscal regime should also be considered as a key element influencing investment decisions. Therefore, as highlighted in the section on taxation, several measures, both general and sector-specific, could be adopted to improve the regime.

General measures related to taxation such as ensuring competitive rates, transparency, simplicity and stability and a well-functioning regime are important factors that investors take into account when choosing a location for their projects. For example, this report recommends reviewing the corporate income tax rate, harmonizing the withholding taxes and eliminating the charge on CIF imports. It also proposes providing high quality administrative services to large investors to help them deal with the tax system's requirements. In addition, Sierra Leone should negotiate DTTs with key partners and, in particular, finalize a DTT with ECOWAS to fully reap the benefits of regional integration.

To stimulate the agro-processing and export manufacturing activities, two sectors identified as priorities for the government, specific measures should be adopted. This includes a low or zero corporate income tax on exports by industries in these sectors (income on domestic sales would be subject to the standard tax rate). This measure could be accompanied by additional incentives to encourage beneficial investment impact such as large-scale employment and self-provision of infrastructure.

---

[60] MAGS was established in 1956 as a limited liability company. In 1979, the government acquired 51 per cent of its shares and in February 1994 the National Provisional Ruling Council Decree No. 2 of February 1994 expropriated the remaining 49 per cent private shares of 14 private shareholders (PWC, 2007).

Adopting a competitive, transparent and simple tax system could also contribute to dealing with the large informal sector. Not only will this aspect have positive impacts on state revenues but it will also make local businesses more attractive to foreign firms and thus enable linkages and spillover effects on the local economy.

## b.   Introducing supportive measures for infrastructure development

Sierra Leone is confronted with many infrastructure challenges that, if not addressed, will continue to significantly hamper investment, economic growth, poverty reduction and ultimately sustainable development. The limited infrastructures deteriorated during the war and significant efforts are needed to rehabilitate them. Furthermore, the war also halted the development of new infrastructure, leaving the country well behind in terms of meeting the basic needs of its growing population. As a result, there is a lack of electricity, water, transport and telecommunications infrastructures.

To increase the supply of electricity and before considering privatizing it, a top priority is to rehabilitate the NPA under a management contract. At the same time, a task force, backed by strong political support, should ensure that the power sector strategy is effectively implemented and that capacity-building activities are undertaken to strengthen the NPA.

While a general review and modernization of the legal framework is needed, some specific laws need immediate attention. For example, there are initiatives from private investors to build transport infrastructure, which highlights the need for a regulatory framework to deal with PPPs in this area. This would also require proper coordination with existing sector laws, policy management and institutional capacity. International experience shows that countries can benefit from such projects if they are governed by clear and stable legal bases as well as sufficient technical and institutional capacity. Countries such as Guinea and Senegal have already dealt with legal frameworks and agreements for private companies' involvement in developing transport infrastructure. A review of such experiences and other approaches is needed to carefully consider the best options available to Sierra Leone.

Furthermore, to proceed with the privatization of port services under a landlord approach, adjustments are required to the Ports Act (1964), the Cargo Clearing and Forwarding Act (1974) and the Sierra Leone Maritime Administration Act (2000). The planned overall changes for the port sector also provide an opportunity for institutional reorganization and sector regulation. The privatization of the airport ground handling services would require that the government update the Sierra Leone Airport Authority Act (1988) and take measures to liquidate the SNA.

## c.   Simplifying requirements for establishing a business

The analysis presented in this chapter indicates that recent changes have improved the procedures for establishing a business. However, there are areas such as modernization of laws and regulations, simplification of procedures, transparency and coordination that are required to further enhance conditions for doing business. To this end, it is recommended to:
*   Effectively implement the new Companies Act in order to use a modern and clear framework to regulate business;
*   Give the appropriate tools and means to the Corporate Affairs Commission so that it can fulfil its mandate of simplifying business registration requirements and streamlining licensing permits;
*   Review the licence structure to maintain those licences that are necessary to protect health, consumers and workers, and the environment and to ensure safety;
*   Assign to SLIEPA a role to facilitate the registration of businesses.

As mentioned previously, simplifying the business registration procedures could also contribute to shifting business from the informal to the formal sector. In addition to increasing revenues, this could also provide a better base to enhance linkages between foreign and national firms.

### d.    Improving trade facilitation

Major deficiencies persist in the way Sierra Leone organizes its import and export activities. Adding transaction costs negatively affects competitiveness and discourages FDI. It is therefore urgent to take measures to correct this situation.

In terms of the regulatory framework, the government should put in place a new Customs Law and finalize its related regulations. This would allow the customs authority to apply the WTO Agreement on Customs Valuation and use the Harmonized Commodity Description and Coding System of tariff nomenclature. It would also permit a risk management approach for customs inspection. Furthermore, the adoption of the customs information system currently being set up by UNCTAD (ASYCUDA++) will improve customs revenue collection, contribute to combating fraud and trafficking of prohibited and restricted goods, and strengthen statistical information on foreign trade transactions. In addition, it is recommended to introduce a modern and harmonized customs procedure to support the transit of goods from neighbouring countries, and a duty drawback regime to allow businesses to rapidly obtain inputs at world prices.

### e.    Facilitating the attraction of skilled workers

Among the many challenges Sierra Leone faces, the lack of educated and skilled labour ranks high. Investors have difficulty finding workers with specific skills. This is the case for example, at varying degrees, in investment projects in mining, telecommunications, light manufacturing and tourism. While there are different ways to deal with the problem, addressing the shortcomings of the regulatory framework is central. In addition to easing labour market rigidities, measures should be taken to attract workers from abroad.

In this context, a review of the process to give work permits to foreigners is needed, with a view to simplifying and clarifying it. The elements to be considered are: the criteria used to issue permits both to workers and their dependants; the institutional structure with responsibilities for these permits, including the Work Permit Committee; the timeline and processing period for applications; and the availability of information for investors and workers, including in the diaspora.

### f.    Modernizing outdated regulations

The analysis presented in this chapter has clearly shown that the legal framework in Sierra Leone is for a large part outdated and not suited to meet the current and emerging needs of the country. While recognizing that the modernization of the regulatory framework is time consuming and requires substantial human and financial capacity, this report recommends focusing efforts on some of its key aspects.

Against this background, efforts should be made to: replace existing laws with new legislation concerning electricity, port services, land registration rights and tourism; review and update legislation regarding mining and fisheries; and create new laws for the operation of activities under privately developed transport infrastructure (e.g. mining transportation projects), commercial courts, competition and bankruptcy.

By addressing these issues, the Government of Sierra Leone will put in place the regulatory and institutional framework that is required to attract and facilitate FDI. Recognizing the human, financial and institutional capacity constraints the country faces, these actions should be taken in a coherent and sequenced manner. Strengthening institutions and improving capacity for policy management should focus on the mining sector, given its prominent role in terms of attracting FDI, including that of the diaspora. In addition, the support from the international community through technical assistance activities will be essential to move this agenda forward. Chapter III of this report presents an overall strategy to foster a new environment to attract FDI into Sierra Leone and provides some sense of prioritization for the implementation of the measures proposed in this chapter.

## CHAPTER III

# TAPPING INTERNATIONAL BEST PRACTICES TO STIMULATE INVESTMENT IN SIERRA LEONE

## A.  Introduction

This chapter proposes a FDI attraction strategy that incorporates best practices tailored to the needs of Sierra Leone. While the strategy is designed to attract investors globally, regional investors are the ones most likely to invest in Sierra Leone in the short to medium term. This assumption is reflected in the strategy, which also seeks to build on the role that regional investors can play in developing Sierra Leone's image as an attractive location for investment.

Taking into account the government's development objectives and targeted sectors (i.e. agriculture, transportation and power) as well as the constraints to FDI attraction, the recommendations are articulated around two scenarios. Since the end of the war, Sierra Leone has benefited from a significant number of reforms and development programme activities. Notwithstanding these activities, it is realistic to anticipate that the constraints to attract FDI outlined in chapters I and II, such as inadequate infrastructure, limited capacity in terms of human capital and government administration, an underdeveloped private sector and a frail judicial system may not all be addressed concurrently or comprehensively in the near future. In this context, the two scenarios provide a dynamic approach for the implementation of a FDI attraction strategy and are based on the following:

- Under scenario 1, reforms and progress in addressing the most serious constraints to FDI attraction proceed at a relatively moderate pace, similar to what has happened in the recent past. For example, major improvements in infrastructure have yet to be achieved. Education and skills, although increasing, are not sufficient to meet the needs of investors and the capacity of the government continues to be problematic, slowing important regulatory reforms;
- Under scenario 2, the main constraints to attracting FDI are addressed forcefully and with success, representing a significant break from past trends and experiences. Significant progress is achieved in providing power and transport infrastructure, bringing Sierra Leone to at least a regional standard. The labour force is better trained and the institutional capacity of the government has significantly increased. In addition, the country benefits from a regulatory framework conducive to FDI, the justice system begins to offer a reliable mechanism to settle investment disputes and enforce contracts and corruption has abated dramatically.

## B.  Assessment of FDI potential

Investment by nationals is one of the main driving forces of economic transformation and plays an important role in a country's ability to attract FDI. Total investment by national entities (private and public) frequently correlates closely with relative levels of FDI inflows. A country successful at attracting FDI is typically one that has a high level of investment by its own entrepreneurs. The developmental benefits from national investment such as a dynamic private sector, skilled labour force, better infrastructure and a wider network of suppliers are attributes foreign investors seek when selecting a location to conduct business (UNCTAD, 2007a).

Some of the reforms proposed in this report are specifically aimed at promoting and attracting foreign investment. Many measures, however, would benefit foreign and national investors alike as they would result in an overall improvement in the investment climate. Although it is extremely difficult to assess in any precise and accurate manner the level of FDI inflows that Sierra Leone could expect to attract in the medium term, it is important to set realistic expectations about future levels of FDI inflows.

**Figure III.1. Potential net non-mining FDI inflows 2008–2020 and comparator countries**
(In millions of dollars)

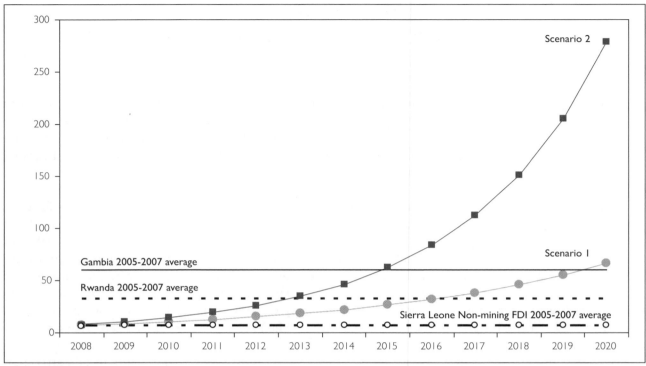

*Source*: UNCTAD estimates.

In order to provide orders of magnitude of what would be in the realm of possibilities in terms of FDI inflows under the two scenarios, some simple rules of thumb have been used to compute estimates for the period 2008–2020 (figure III.1). Although no disaggregate data exist,[61] it is estimated that non-mining FDI inflows in Sierra Leone have represented around 10 per cent of total FDI flows over the past few years, equivalent to around 3 per cent of gross fixed capital formation (GFCF). GFCF, in turn, has recovered from less than 7 per cent of GDP in 2001 to around 17 per cent in 2007 as a result of an increase in FDI and a resurgence in investment by national entities (public and private sectors).

The forecast for non-mining FDI inflows for the medium term is built around three key variables: (1) nominal GDP growth (dollar terms); (2) the level of investment by national entities (as a percentage of GDP); and (3) the relative level of non-mining FDI (as a percentage of GFCF). Scenario 1 assumes that nominal GDP grows at 8 per cent per annum,[62] that national investment increases to 18 per cent of GDP by 2020 and that non-mining FDI flows rise to about 6.5 per cent of GFCF, which is about half the level achieved by the LDCs on average in the period 2003–2007.

Scenario 2, in turn, reflects the more optimistic and ambitious reform agenda it presumes. Nominal GDP grows at 11 per cent per annum and national investment increases to 24 per cent of GDP by 2020. This higher level of national investment and more significant achievements in the reform process are also assumed to result in better performance in terms of relative non-mining FDI inflows, which, in the simulation, are projected to grow to almost 15 per cent of GFCF by 2020, close to the LDCs' average.

The estimates indicated that under a continuation of the moderate pace of reforms of the past few years, Sierra Leone could aim at attracting around $60 million of non-mining FDI inflows per year by 2020.

---

[61] On the issue of lack of data, Sierra Leone could benefit from training programmes provided by UNCTAD aiming at reinforcing its statistical capacity. This would help the country to collect and disseminate data, better evaluate the impact of foreign investments, prepare forecasts on the potential of FDI inflows and thus formulate sounder and better FDI attraction strategies.

[62] Real GDP growth is assumed at 5 per cent under scenario 1 and 8 per cent under scenario 2 over the entire forecast period.

Although this is a relatively modest amount, it is far from negligible as it excludes all investments in mining. The estimate is based on relatively conservative assumptions regarding overall economic performance, but achieving the underlying assumptions would require significant improvements in terms of investment by national entities and FDI attraction. It would thus require sustained progress in the reform agenda.

Under the bolder, bigger and more successful reform agenda assumed under scenario 2, Sierra Leone could aim at attracting more than $200 million of non-mining FDI inflows per year by 2020. Attaining such levels presumes strong and sustained progress in the reform drive, well above what has been achieved over the past decade. It builds on a virtuous circle of structural reforms, an improved investment climate, better infrastructure and a higher skills level, led by a sharp increase in investment by nationals.

Consolidating the peace process and ensuring stability and security in Sierra Leone are necessary conditions for either scenario to materialize. It is widely recognized that post-conflict peace is fragile. Research results show that the average risk for a post-conflict country to revert to conflict is typically high (for example, Collier *et al.* (2006) estimate this risk to be 40 per cent within the decade).

While many factors can explain conflicts (e.g. political repression, ethnic and religious divisions), economic characteristics play a very important role. For example, empirical research shows that dependence on primary commodity exports, low growth and incomes are all significant and powerful predictors of violent conflicts (Collier, 2006). Recognizing this fact clearly calls for improved economic conditions in Sierra Leone. Against this background, the global economic slowdown constitutes an important threat to the peace process. If the current situation diverts attention of the international community to forcefully supporting the development of Sierra Leone, the risks of conflicts will inevitably increase. Therefore, this points to the need and importance for all actors, including the donor community and the government, to keep the focus on effectively addressing the economic and social challenges Sierra Leone faces.

## C. Scenario 1: A moderate overall pace of reforms

In formulating initiatives to attract FDI, the sizeable development challenges facing Sierra Leone must be acknowledged. Thus, taking into account the drain on government resources to address these important challenges, this first scenario assumes a slow to moderate pace of reforms and the persistence of constraints in terms of infrastructure, human capital, administrative capacity and the regulatory framework.

### 1. FDI potential remains limited

The recommendations of scenario 1 build upon the measures emanating from the analysis of the regulatory investment framework (chapter II). They are complemented by more general measures affecting investment flows. Implementing these recommendations requires relatively few financial and human resources as well as limited legislative changes and could be completed within a 12- to 18-month period. These recommendations would not drastically change the fundamentals to attract FDI, but as near-term solutions, they would help maintain the current FDI inflows and build the foundation to attract higher levels in the future.

Under this scenario, FDI would continue to be concentrated in the mining sector. As a result, spillovers and developmental impacts, such as job creation, linkages and knowledge transfer would be limited. Similarly, the contribution of FDI to economic diversification and infrastructure development would continue to be limited. This leaves an important role for donors to play in terms of ensuring that basic infrastructures are gradually built to support economic and social development.

### 2. FDI attraction and promotion strategy

The underdeveloped infrastructure, the small domestic market and the lack of export experience outside the mining sector indicate that Sierra Leone would be, initially, an unlikely destination for investment

> ## Box III.1. Nigeria and South Africa as powerhouses of intra-African investment
>
> Intra-African investment is increasing. At the same time, traditional investment in mining is shifting to include other sectors. Knowledge of and adaptability to local conditions are among the factors explaining this shift; the transfer of skill is another. The two main sources of investment, Nigeria and South Africa, have been effective in dealing with management and other factors characterizing investing in African countries.
>
> Nigeria contributes more than 50 per cent to the overall GDP of West Africa. The Joint Development Zone, an initiative between Equatorial Guinea, Nigeria and Sao Tome and Principe, may create a trend in more forcefully promoting regional investment.
>
> There are several Nigerian investment projects in Sierra Leone in banking, insurance and the petroleum industry (distribution). The United Bank for Africa and Zenith Bank, two of Nigeria's largest commercial banks, have started operations in Sierra Leone as part of their strategy to establish branches across Africa. While not active in Sierra Leone, Nigerian investments could target projects such as sugar refineries as well as transport and infrastructure. In this regard, Nigeria's Dangote Group, which controls much of Nigeria's commodities trade, is expanding its operations in West Africa in areas such as the manufacture of consumer and food products including sugar, flour, salt and pastas. The Dangote Group has also made important investments in the cement industry, telecommunications and fertilizer processing. Other interests include commercial real estate complexes and truck transportation services. The Dagote Group constitutes a potential investor for Sierra Leone.
>
> South Africa is leading in terms of intra-African investment. In the past, South African investment focused almost exclusively on the extractive sector. However, the country has diversified its projects in the service-oriented industries including investments in telecommunications, information technology, banking, media, retail and advertising. There are 10 South African TNCs among the top 100 TNCs from developing countries in sectors such as computer-related business, appliances sectors and motor vehicles. If Sierra Leone adopts a conducive environment for investment, they could become ideal potential investors in the country.
>
> *Source:* UNCTAD (2008b).

from large TNCs. However, regional investors, in particular from ECOWAS countries, may be interested in doing business in the country. Their familiarity with investment conditions and opportunities in the region make them an ideal target for investment promotion activities from SLIEPA. They may also be well suited to undertake the type of investments to serve the small, but growing, domestic market in Sierra Leone (box III.1).

From Sierra Leone's perspective, investors from the region could contribute to increased employment and training. Their presence could also be used as a launching ground for future expansion of FDI from other source countries. Sierra Leone could use the success of these investors to demonstrate the changing landscape of investment. By developing success stories, Sierra Leone would gain credibility and could then more easily expand its investor targeting to include investors from all of Africa and globally.

Under scenario 1, efforts to attract regional investors should focus on measures to facilitate investment. These measures include: (i) ensuring the adoption of basic legal measures to improve the investment framework; (ii) providing FDI facilitation services; (iii) providing aftercare services; (iv) easing entry visa requirements; and (v) improving Sierra Leone's image through a limited programme of investment promotion.

### a. Ensuring the adoption of basic legal measures to improve the investment framework

Under scenario 1, a number of measures should be taken to improve the investment framework and lay the foundation for using FDI to stimulate economic growth and sustainable development. These measures should be adopted within a short period of time, preferably before the end of 2010. This is the criteria guiding the selection of recommendations for scenario I. These recommendations are articulated around five out of the six main areas of action from chapter II:

- Establishing a competitive and effective fiscal regime;
- Introducing supportive measures for infrastructure development;
- Simplifying requirements for establishing a business;
- Improving trade facilitation;
- Facilitating the attraction of skilled workers.

The establishment of a competitive and effective fiscal regime should begin with the introduction of the VAT as planned for 2009. The government should also remove restrictions on the utilization of loss carry-forward and review the advance tax payments. In addition, withholding taxes on payments to service contractors, royalties, interests and dividends should be reduced and harmonized, and the same income tax rate should be applied to resident and non-resident small business owners. There are also specific actions that should be taken to improve the conditions for foreign investment in the mining sector. In addition to reducing the corporate tax rate for this sector, there is a need to review the fiscal terms of mining leases (chapter II).

With respect to supportive measures for infrastructure development, a few essential steps can be undertaken under scenario I to prepare the ground for a longer-term programme that will deal with infrastructure constraints more in depth. The government should draft the laws required to administer the involvement of the private sector in the transport and energy sectors. These laws need to take into account sectoral issues that affect transport and electricity to ensure coordination and consistency.[63] In particular, a decision should be made on the liquidation of the SNA to improve investment prospects in airport services. Furthermore, a task force should be put in place, in accordance with the Energy Sector Strategy Note of 2007, to deal with critical issues related to the electricity supply. This task force should be responsible for the implementation of the Power Sector Reform Strategy and Action Plan that have been prepared. Among its responsibilities, the task force should ensure the proper functioning of the NPA and define the regulatory framework of the "Special Purpose Company".

While the simplification of the requirements to establish a business may necessitate additional time, a first priority is the effective implementation of the new Companies Act and the adequate utilization of the Corporate Affairs Commission. This would ensure that modern and clearer regulations for business are effectively used and ultimately speed up the start-up process.

Sierra Leone can begin addressing issues related to trade facilitation by approving a new Customs Law that includes the WTO Agreement on Customs Valuation. The efficiency of import and export activities could be greatly improved by eliminating the use of PSI procedures, reference values, deposit payment requirements and bank guarantees for the granting of clearance permits.

The contribution of foreign workers in terms of investment and economic growth is well documented. Developed countries such as Canada, Ireland or the United States have long benefited from this type of labour input. More recently, developing countries, such as Mauritius or Singapore, have also realized the benefits foreign workers could bring to their economy and, in this context, adopted accommodating immigration laws to help businesses hire skilled workers from other countries. As companies compete globally to attract skilled workers, it is critical to design conducive entry conditions and labour policies. There are different ways to achieve this result (box III.2). Sierra Leone, though at an early stage of such process, should to a minimum ensure that foreign investors are not discouraged by a lengthy and costly process to get the skills required to run their businesses.

---

[63] For example, such issues include mining, land and tourism. In the mining sector, this is critical as legal disputes over licence rights have already prevented important private firms' transport projects.

> ## Box III.2. Approaches to attract foreign skills
>
> There are different approaches adopted by countries to attract foreign skills including:
>
> **Human capital.** It is aimed at increasing the stock of skilled human resources over the long term. This includes permanent residence as an incentive and full mobility in the labour market. Implementing clear criteria and specific admission policies are key successful characteristics of effective programmes.
>
> **Labour market needs.** This is the most common programme adopted in many countries with the objective of providing a solution to cyclical shortages for skills in the labour market. It is usually made possible through the temporary admission of foreign workers with the requisite experience and qualifications. There is flexibility for the length of stay with a time-bound character of the admission, without settlement of the worker and family.
>
> **Business incentives.** These aim to encourage trade and foreign investments by facilitating the entry and stay of investors, executives and managers, including their family members. Some countries offer permanent residence status to investors who bring in a minimum amount of capital and employ a certain number of workers. Most countries simply offer facilitated temporary admission.
>
> **Academic background.** The objective is to draw talents from the pool of foreign students graduating from educational institutions and encouraging them to work or do research.
>
> These approaches are not mutually exclusive and many countries use them in combination. Optimal policies are usually based on targeting the specific goals they seek to maximize. There seems to be a shift in these programmes from simply easing restrictions (facilitation) to offering incentives (e.g. lower income taxes). The removal of restrictions (e.g. quotas on sectors, occupations or firms; short duration of work permits; labour market certification; minimum salaries; restrictions on changing employers; restrictions on the employment of spouses; limits to extension of permits) is a key requirement in reform efforts and this is manifested in the fact that countries are increasingly seeking to exempt highly skilled workers from various forms of such restrictions.
>
> *Source:* Abella (2006).

Against this background, the shortage of human capital in Sierra Leone could be eased by reviewing the criteria and process to allocate work permits to foreigners. For instance, unifying legally the residence and work permits ("work/residence permit") and giving work authorization to dependents under certain conditions are promising avenues. The process and criteria guiding the allocation of permits should also be made widely available through, for example, the Internet.

In addition, given the important number of Sierra Leoneans in the diaspora, measures to attract them back to the country should be adopted. In this respect, a recent initiative by the diaspora has taken the form of the Direct Expatriate Nationals Investment. Recognizing the potential of the diaspora as a pool of human resources and a source of financing,[64] Direct Expatriate Nationals Investment intends to mobilize expatriates to invest in state-owned enterprises in the context of the ongoing privatization process. This programme, if well managed and further developed, is an opportunity to stimulate the economy and to spread know-how in the country, while creating at the same time a culture of ownership.

Ultimately however, the above-mentioned measures are short-term solutions; education spending will be the pivotal factor in increasing the number of skilled workers in Sierra Leone.

### b.   Providing FDI facilitation services

As the investment promotion agency, SLIEPA should be the coordinating office for all investment projects. Initially, SLIEPA should focus on providing a small number of critical services for investors and

---

[64] Mainly through remittances up to now.

**Figure III.2. Illustration of the Sierra Leone Internet portal**

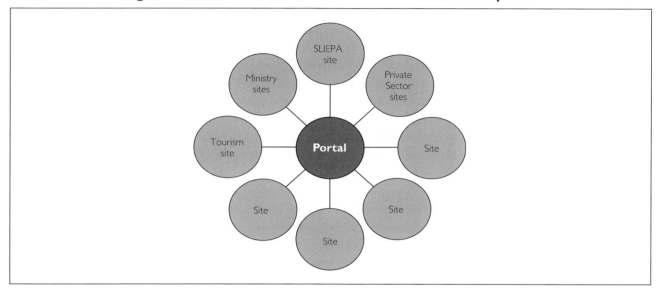

avoid promising a "one-stop shop"[65] (scenario 2). Implementing a one-stop shop under scenario I would overtax the resources of other agencies. To effectively implement the concept, SLIEPA would better serve potential investors as a reliable reference point, providing assistance in meeting procedural requirements and facilitating meetings within the business community.

To facilitate access to information while promoting the new image of the country, a Sierra Leone Web portal should be developed. The World Bank, FIAS and DFID are providing support to SLIEPA and the activities proposed under this scenario complement those of their programme.

As a portal, the website would act as the hub to the various private sector groups and public sector agencies (figure III.2). The content of the portal would not be limited to image-building and promotional aspects of Sierra Leone but would act as a gateway to other information on Sierra Leone. This task should be undertaken as an integrated effort, in coordination with all public entities involved (tourism, government ministries, the private sector, etc). SLIEPA should act as the coordinator and manage the portal's content.

A well-designed, maintained and marketed SLIEPA Internet site is central to its facilitation efforts. In addition to hard copy formats available in its offices, SLIEPA should provide all pertinent information regarding investing in Sierra Leone on its website, including:
- Logistical information on visiting Sierra Leone and the services SLIEPA can offer in coordinating investor visits (visa information, airport pickup, meeting planning, etc.);
- Information on investment projects and opportunities, including promotional materials for selected sectors, should be available online. Initially, the main focus would be on promoting the potential of the mining sector. Subsequently, other promotional materials for specific sectors would be developed according to progress made to improve conditions in those sectors;
- Relevant laws and regulations should be provided, including the principal laws and regulations affecting business activities and specific sector provisions and tax information (developed in cooperation with the National Revenue Authority);
- SLIEPA should facilitate access to financing by leveraging Sierra Leone's partnerships with development organizations both in the country and in the region. For example, using the ECOWAS Private Sector Regional Initiative, a case can be made for investment from the ECOWAS Bank for Investment

---

[65] The term "one-stop shop" implies that all procedural requirements and processing are handled within one office.

and Development (box III.3) such as public-private partnership funding. Other sources with similar programmes include the African Development Bank, the African Union Development Fund and various initiatives of other donors for SME development.

In addition to the facilitation services SLIEPA provides, there is also the need to maintain an investor tracking database. The system should be designed so that SLIEPA can track an investor through out the entire "investment cycle". SLIEPA should monitor investor enquiries, visits, areas of interest, realized investment and any additional source of investment including re-investment. The website can be a useful tool in helping SLIEPA to develop its database. Analytics of users can help improve the site's usability and investor targeting activities. Through short online surveys, SLIEPA can begin creating a profile of potential investors.

In Sierra Leone, communicating with persons outside of the country can be a challenge. SLIEPA should dedicate some of its office space to providing a comfortable and well-organized business centre for its clients. The amenities offered at the SLIEPA offices should include free wireless Internet for its clients by providing a password to a secure connection. Offering printing and copying should also be considered, although any regulatory, legislative, marketing or informative materials should be available in both soft and hard format. As Sierra Leone's communication infrastructure develops, the centre will be less important, but at present it can be a useful facilitation measure. It also has the benefit of being relatively low cost as it uses the resources already needed for SLIEPA personnel.

There are programmes SLIEPA can implement that will add value to their services, particularly those related to facilitating meetings within the business community. The Sierra Leone Business Forum presents an opportunity for investors (domestic and foreign) to engage the government in discussion on topics of concern to them. For the purposes of SLIEPA, the forum could also provide an important contact point for facilitating a particular investor's visit and arranging meetings with investors in Sierra Leone. Therefore, SLIEPA should cultivate the forum as a resource and work to establish a single contact point within the forum who would assist SLIEPA in these activities.

---

**Box III.3. ECOWAS Private Sector Regional Initiatives**

In 2007, ECOWAS established the Private Sector Department to promote cross-border investments, joint venture businesses and small and medium enterprises, and improve the regional business climate. These objectives seek to foster a dynamic and diversified regional economy through a better integrated regional market. This includes:

- Facilitating the involvement of the private sector in the regional integration process through support to regional private sector institutions and creation of relevant new ones. Promoting harmony and synergy among the activities of these institutions and facilitating consultations;
- Promoting the development of a viable regional capital market with strong linkages in all member States to facilitate the mobilization of investment capital and wealth creation;
- Facilitating public-private partnerships and the establishment of multinational joint ventures and community enterprises to foster employment and sustainable inclusive growth in the region;
- Encouraging West African entrepreneurs to develop and maintain links with diaspora groups, relevant continental and international bodies and South–South entities to attract investment.

Under this initiative, the West African Power Pool has developed a number of projects for countries in the region to increase electricity supply, notably in Benin, Burkina Faso, Ghana, Mali, Nigeria and Togo. If successful, this initiative could provide impetus to extend cooperation to countries such as Liberia and Sierra Leone.

*Source:* ECOWAS Secretariat.

### c.    Providing aftercare and policy advocacy services

Enhancing established investors' satisfaction with their decision to invest in Sierra Leone and encouraging these investors to expand operations or move up the value chain is an important function of the investment promotion agency (UNCTAD, 2008a). Commonly called aftercare, these activities can be more important when there are only a few investors or, in times of economic slowdown, where investors are not seeking to expand into new locations but instead may upgrade existing operations. Under scenario 1, the resources may not be available to pursue an extensive aftercare programme. However, there are activities that should be undertaken that would help prepare the agency for larger programmes and services provided as part of its aftercare initiatives.

One of the initiatives SLIEPA should begin implementing is a programme to foster linkages between FDI and domestic suppliers of goods and services. In concert with building the investor database, SLIEPA should have the ability to sort foreign firms by areas of business. During this ongoing process, SLIEPA should begin to append demand requirements from the domestic economy and domestic suppliers of goods and services that have corresponding supplies. Initially, SLIEPA can focus on the mining sector where most FDI is concentrated.

Nevertheless, it is more likely that linkages will take place if local businesses are registered in the formal sector and capable of effectively supplying foreign firms. It is thus advisable for the government to encourage and assist in the development of SMEs as they could become key players in the economy. In this regard, they should be encouraged to participate in training programmes offered by EMPRETEC centres in the region, such as Ghana and Nigeria.[66] Such training would help potential business people acquire the knowledge necessary to start their company and possibly become effective suppliers to TNCs. In the longer run, as developed in scenario 2 below, Sierra Leone could plan to create its own EMPRETEC centre.

Another important aspect of SLIEPA's role is policy advocacy, a mechanism through which investors can respond to policies affecting FDI. Effective policy advocacy requires creating a simple but effective coalition with business organizations. It is therefore recommended that an Investment Promotion Committee, led by SLIEPA in coordination with the Sierra Leone Business Forum, be put in place to encourage communication and coordination among all of the government agencies that have responsibility for the development or execution of investment policy, in cooperation with other private sector stakeholders. Inter-ministerial coordination and close consultation with the private sector are to be encouraged. As part of this outreach, it is recommended that an Investors' Round Table with international and local business leaders be held. This could be done through the use of the Business Forum to develop a regular series of round tables with international and local business leaders to discuss Sierra Leone's FDI issues.

SLIEPA's success will be dependant upon its organizational soundness. This includes adequate staffing and budget support. Furthermore, the staff will require training to become effective. At this stage, SLIEPA is in a good position to focus on training, gather investor information and begin formalizing programmes with the domestic private sector and the public sector. In this regard, the adoption, in 2009, of a client charter is very positive step forward. This is indeed a valuable tool to promoting a customer service approach and constitutes a core element of good governance for a public institution. In addition to outlining the vision and mission of the institution, the charter also gives information about the range and fees of the various services provided.

### d.    Easing entry visa requirements

A primary consideration in attracting FDI is the challenge of increasing the pool of potential investors. The first interaction potential investors have with the Sierra Leonean administration is frequently at its embassies during the visa process. Business visitors wishing to enter the country must obtain a business

---

[66] EMPRETEC is a capacity-building programme of UNCTAD aimed at promoting entrepreneurial skills for SMEs. It helps them become more innovative and competitive and also encourages beneficial business linkages with TNCs. A centre is set up at the request of the country with the support of UNCTAD. These centres then become independent entities.

visa. The current exception for ECOWAS citizens is a positive step in making Sierra Leone more accessible to regional investors, as they are the primary target audience in the near term. There is an opportunity, however, to widen the appeal of Sierra Leone to investors from other potential source countries.

The current reciprocal policy towards visas and visa fees does not help Sierra Leone attract sufficient and beneficial FDI to reach its development objectives. Reciprocal entry treatment is a policy that hinders investors' attempts to explore Sierra Leone's potential, and assessing fees on the basis of nationality creates an additional administrative burden and presents a challenge in training embassy personnel. For example, the fees for persons travelling from the United Kingdom and the United States vary from $70 to $431 depending on whether the visa is for single or multiple entry, while Canadian visas range from $72 to $144.[67] The rates are somewhat extreme in comparison to other countries in the region and within Africa (table III.1).

**Table III.1. Visa requirements of countries in the region and other African countries**

| Regional | Number of countries exempted | Economies exempted[a] | Cost for single entry business visa[b] |
|---|---|---|---|
| *Sierra Leone* | *14* | *ECOWAS* | *range $40–$131* |
| Liberia | 14 | ECOWAS | range $70–$131 |
| Nigeria | 14 | ECOWAS | range $25–$139 |
| Guinea | 14 | ECOWAS | $100 |
| Gambia | 16 | ECOWAS, United Kingdom, Australia | $100 |
| Ghana | 20 | ECOWAS, Egypt, Hong Kong (China), Kenya, Mauritius, Singapore, Zimbabwe, | $50 |
| **Other comparators** | | | |
| Kenya | 37 | Botswana, Brunei Darussalam, Gambia, Ghana, Jamaica, Lesotho, Malawi, Mauritius, Namibia, Sierra Leone, Singapore, Swaziland, Uganda, United Republic of Tanzania, Zambia, Zimbabwe | $50 |
| Rwanda | 11 | Burundi, Canada, Germany, Hong Kong (China), Kenya, South Africa, Sweden, Uganda, United States, United Kingdom | $60 |
| South Africa | 64 | More than 15 EU countries, Australia, Brazil, Canada, Japan, Singapore, Mozambique, Republic of Korea, Thailand, Turkey, Zambia | $47 |
| Uganda | 36 | COMESA, Gambia, Sierra Leone, Singapore | $50 |

[a] Exempted means no visa required. The exemptions generally cover stays of 30 days or less and 90 days or less.
[b] In several cases countries do not distinguish between business visas and tourist visas, nor multiple or single entry.
COMESA: Angola, Burundi, Comoros, Eritrea, Kenya, Madagascar, Malawi, Mauritius, Rwanda, Seychelles, Swaziland, United Republic of Tanzania, Zambia, Zimbabwe.
*Sources*: Embassy websites and embassy personnel.

In the near term, there are three recommendations that will assist Sierra Leone in balancing the desire to create a welcoming environment for genuine investors against the need to limit exposure to foreign entrants whose motives are suspect.

**1. SLIEPA should work closely with the Ministry of Internal Affairs to create and maintain a priority list of countries, which are important sources of FDI, that would be exempt from visa requirements**

---

[67] Sierra Leone Embassy, Washington DC.

A priority list of exempt countries is a measure that would help potential investors from countries outside the ECOWAS region to visit Sierra Leone. Table III.I provides a point of reference by highlighting the policies of countries in the region and throughout Africa. Using important sectors such as mining combined with countries that present low risk but high investment outflows (table III.2), an initial list of priority countries has been developed.

### Table III.2. 2008 FDI outflows from selected economies
(In millions of dollars)

| | Outflows | | Outflows |
|---|---|---|---|
| **Africa** | **9 309** | **EU** | **836 573** |
| Egypt | 1 920 | France | 220 046 |
| Morocco | 369 | Germany | 156 457 |
| Gabon | 96 | United Kingdom | 111 411 |
| Mauritius | 52 | Spain | 77 317 |
| Kenya | 44 | Belgium | 68 278 |
| **West Africa (ECOWAS)** | **1 389** | **Other economies with high outflows** | |
| Guinea | 694 | United States | 311 796 |
| Liberia | 382 | Japan | 128 020 |
| Nigeria | 299 | Switzerland | 86 295 |
| Senegal | 9 | Canada | 77 667 |
| | | Hong Kong, China | 59 920 |

*Source:* UNCTAD (2009).

The following are important source countries for FDI and are strategically important to Sierra Leone in sectors such as mining and tourism. At the same time, they present a low exposure to illegal immigration. As such, they are good candidates for the initial priority list.

- Australia
- Canada
- China
- EU countries
- Japan
- Libyan Arab Jamahiriya
- Republic of Korea
- Russian Federation
- Saudi Arabia
- Singapore
- South Africa
- Switzerland
- United States

The priority list should be reassessed periodically as investment promotion efforts are refined, FDI targets expand and sources of FDI change. This would ensure that the list remains relevant as Sierra Leone's FDI attraction strategy evolves. As the list is reviewed, the Ministry of Internal Affairs and SLIEPA should conduct a more stringent analysis of priority countries. For example, although it is well known that investors in the mining sector originate largely from Australia, Canada and Switzerland, recently companies from Mexico have appeared as top TNCs in the sector.[68] Of the top 100 TNCs from developing countries, in terms of foreign assets, two firms from the Republic of Korea are at the top in the electronics and motor vehicles industries. In food and beverage, three companies from Mexico and three from Singapore make the top 100 list. These and other parameters should be used to develop a deeper analysis as the list is assessed and resources become available.

### 2. Simplify the fee structure and reduce fees

For those countries not on the priority list, a flat fee should be considered, regardless of visa type. The amount should cover administrative costs only. This approach avoids the pitfall of using visa fees as a revenue stream and as a result failing to capture the more lucrative revenue generated by visitors and investment.

---

[68] Cemex of Mexico is ranked 71 on the World Investment Reports list of World's Top 100 Non-Financial TNCs ranked by foreign assets (UNCTAD, 2008b).

A more streamlined approach to visa fees will reduce the administrative burden and allow better information management and facilitate consular services training. One benefit, which may be the most significant, is the investors' enhanced impression of Sierra Leone. Typically, there is a preconception that there will be significant amounts of red tape and bureaucracy to manage in Sierra Leone. A streamlined approach to fees and well-informed personnel will work to dispel the impression and show that Sierra Leone is making strides in its reforms.

### 3. Provide one source of information online and ensure personnel are well versed in the visa structure

The personnel in the embassies and missions are the frontline of Sierra Leone's image. As the first impression is often the basis for all future interactions, it is important that the personnel are knowledgeable about the visa fees and process. A secure, intra-government website could be put in place to provide embassy and consulate personnel with one consistent source for information.

### f.    Improving Sierra Leone's image through a limited programme of investment promotion

In spite of a number of years of peace and political stability, the image of Sierra Leone remains tarnished by the war, leaving a gap between reality and perceptions of the country. In order to attract FDI, the image of Sierra Leone as a peaceful and stable country will need to be promoted. A detailed image-building strategy is beyond the scope of this review; however, there are several recommendations tied to the role of SLIEPA that can be implemented under scenario 1.

As described above, a well-designed, marketed and regularly updated Internet portal could contribute to image-building efforts. SLIEPA should also make use of current materials to initiate a regional marketing campaign to boost Sierra Leone's image and promote investment opportunities. At this stage, where significant reforms have yet to materialize, the promotion should be on a smaller scale. Moving more slowly and with more focus on a few markets will allow SLIEPA to develop the tools necessary for this type of promotion, build capacity and conduct test marketing. Through this approach, SLIEPA can identify what methods and marketing promotions are the most effective for its targeted markets. Focusing on informational meetings with private sector groups to discuss investment opportunities, the campaign could include distribution of materials through embassies, use well-known personalities to speak about the country and develop feature stories for news coverage about Sierra Leone. It can also take the form of larger events such as, for example, the Trade and Investment Forum held in London in November 2009. This highly successful event gathered close to 700 participants, including numerous high-level personalities, and provided an opportunity to present the ambitious reform agenda of the government and the investment opportunities of the country and share the experiences of existing investors in Sierra Leone.

## D.  Scenario 2: Successful reforms significantly improved the investment climate

Scenario 2 provides a strategic vision for what the country could achieve in relation to FDI attraction if it realizes a breakthrough from past performances and sustains major progress in structural reforms over prolonged period of time. Scenario 2 builds upon solutions being found to structural impediments to attracting FDI such as poor infrastructure, inadequate human capital and administrative capacity, and a weak regulatory framework and judicial system. Specifically, this means that:
*   Power supply meets at least the current demand for electricity;
*   Water supply meets existing demand in principal economic centres;
*   Road connectivity to important economic centres is re-established;
*   Private sector activity is increasingly taking place in the formal sector;
*   The judicial system functions well;

- Key public institutions have sufficient capacity;[69]
- A solid regulatory framework is in place;
- Training programmes are provided to improve the skills of the labour force;
- Domestic revenue collection is significantly improved;
- Good governance and social, political and economic stability are maintained;
- Major investment disputes have been resolved.

Getting to the point where such conditions are met would require unprecedented efforts and successes in structural reforms over a prolonged period. It would not only call for a very committed and focused reform drive on behalf of the Government of Sierra Leone, but also for the strong and coordinated support of the international community. The role of the latter is likely to be important in the early phase of the reform drive and would be required, in particular, in the areas of capacity-building and infrastructure development.

A number of suggestions are provided to tackle some of the key structural impediments highlighted above. As reforms in these areas yield results, Sierra Leone would be in a position to put in place more forceful sectoral strategies and initiatives, as well as a more proactive FDI promotional campaign. As noted at the beginning of this chapter, the measures and reforms considered under the two scenarios are not mutually exclusive and should not be considered as substitutes. Frequently, recommendations in scenario 2 build upon the foundation of recommendations in scenario 1.

## 1.   Tackling structural impediments to FDI

### a.   Infrastructure

Sierra Leone's inadequacies in infrastructure will require sizeable investments in the foreseeable future. The needs cover all areas of basic infrastructure, i.e. transport (roads, rail, ports and airports), electricity (generation, transmission, distribution and rural electrification), water (supply and access to clean water, sanitation and water treatment), agriculture infrastructure (irrigation, sanitary and phytosanitary inspection) and telecommunications (telephony and Internet connectivity). A significant part of infrastructure development will have to be covered by public investments. Given the shortage of financial capacity, support from the international community will be crucial in that area. There are also some selected cases in which private investors may be in a position to contribute to infrastructure development. This is already the case, like in most countries in the world, in telecommunications, but could also extend to transport and electricity, given appropriate policies and regulatory frameworks.

Sierra Leone needs to invest heavily in transport infrastructure to begin realizing its development potential and attract FDI. There are several ongoing projects using aid from international donors but the numerous and competing needs (e.g. feeder/main roads, urban/rural roads, airport expansion/a new airport) leave significant room for additional investment from the private sector. Some examples of infrastructure investment needs that have been identified are listed in table III.3.

At present, there is weak coordination to address transport infrastructure needs, including private sector, regional governments and donor initiatives. In this regard, the Ministries of Transportation and Public Works along with SLIEPA should work with the corresponding stakeholders to identify and promote specific investment projects.

Impediments to attracting FDI in infrastructure frequently include delays in project start-ups, contract cancellations, legal disputes, corruption, weak capacity of public entities to structure and design investment projects, and inadequate policy framework. There is evidence that FDI in infrastructure responds positively

---

[69] These entities would include: the National Revenue Authority; the judicial system; Ministries of Mineral Resources, Agriculture, Fisheries, Land, Energy and Power, Finance, Trade, Transport, Public Works; the National Tourism Board; the Law Reform Commission.

to an effective domestic policy and regulatory framework, while weak regulatory institutions engender a strong reluctance to invest (Kirkpatrick et al., 2006). The dispute between African Minerals and London Mining concerning licence rights illustrates this well in the case of Sierra Leone.

**Table III.3. Examples of investment needs in transport**

| Sector | Area of investment | Estimated costs (in thousands of dollars) |
|---|---|---|
| Roads | Class A (primary roads): asphalt cement surface | 667 150 |
| | Class B (secondary roads): double surface treatment | 569 910 |
| | Class B: gravel earth and drainage | 131 245 |
| | 250 km urban street asphalt | 88 250 |
| | Modern traffic management system for Sierra Leone | 10 000 |
| Ports and maritime transport | Tug boat | 4 500 |
| | Pavement and infrastructure on reclaimed land area | 6 000 |
| | Landing sites rehabilitation / development | 10 000 |
| | Dredging waterways | 6 000 |
| Airport | Ground landing equipment | 500 |
| | Metrological unit equipment | 500 |
| | Modern car park / helipad and sea rescue boat house | 800 |
| | Fire and patrol vehicle | 250 |
| | Construction of new runway, terminal building, control tower and NAVAIDS | 25 000 |

*Source:* Ministry of Transport and Aviation (2007).

It is therefore important that Sierra Leone adopts an appropriate policy framework when seeking to attract investment in infrastructure development. Furthermore, Sierra Leone should include developing economies in their targeting efforts related to infrastructure investment. Recently, Hong Kong (China), Malaysia, Singapore and the United Arab Emirates (UNCTAD, 2008b) have become important sources of FDI in infrastructure.

Additional opportunities exist to promote investment in infrastructure in connection with the goals proposed by the ECOWAS regional integration efforts. Moving forward on this front is necessary not only to identify capital and funding possibilities but also to begin addressing the significant weaknesses of the transportation connection with neighbouring countries.

## b.   Port development

Attracting investors in port activity is not only important for increasing investment levels but also to increase overall economic activity and with it further the attractiveness of Sierra Leone as an FDI destination. In West and Central Africa, where intraregional road and air links remain weak, sea transport accounts for up to 90 per cent of foreign trade by volume. Efficient maritime transport is therefore critical to the region's trade and income growth (Harding *et al.*, 2007).

The government has decided that the privatization of the Port of Freetown would take place under a landlord approach (chapter II). It is now strategically important that the concession of the Port of Freetown to private investors be pushed forcefully. The positive effects and importance of a well-functioning port, including a more efficient and cost-effective delivery of imports for the domestic economy and improved transport linkages with the hinterland, should be highlighted.

Ports, as an integral part of the logistics chain, increasingly have to provide value added services beyond the traditional cargo handling functions. Once fully implemented, a new port operation under a landlord approach would be strategic in contributing to the addition of value by promoting new economic activities. They would include linkages to the already approved petroleum exploration, basic but highly labour intensive simple services of ship cleaning and repairing, storage and redistribution of small cargo to regional countries, packaging and preservation facilities for agro- and fishery processing, and other services to maritime transport (e.g. food and fuel supplies).

As a small port in West Africa (box III.4), the Freetown Port can play a role within the West Africa maritime corridor. Although the port is small, if run efficiently and competitively it would have a role to play in decongesting larger ports that need to accommodate larger vessels and cargos. It could increasingly attract small cargos normally destined for Sierra Leone and other small cargos for neighbouring countries. This would also consolidate the role of Freetown with increasingly integrated West Africa and ECOWAS markets.

Given the major reforms and length of time that would be needed to implement a full modernization of the Port of Freetown, expectations should be realistic about the limitations in the short and medium term to position the Port of Freetown for fast operations characterized by a "just in time" supply chain for transportation-dependent operation (e.g. manufacturers, wholesalers, suppliers, shippers and retailers).

---

### Box III.4. The Port of Freetown

The port has traffic of approximately 38,000 tons of exports and 400,000 tons of imports annually. Of the three berths at the largest quay, one has facilities for the discharge of bulk grain using suction and conveyor systems and the loading of bulk palm kernel oil. The other two are used for general cargo. There is also the Kissy Oil Terminal, which provides facilities for the discharge of petroleum products. Overall, and as illustrated in the table, the port is relatively small in comparison to others in the region.

#### Container traffic in West Africa
(In 20-foot equivalent units or TEUs)

| Country | Port | TEUs |
|---|---|---|
| Côte d'Ivoire | Abidjan | 670 000 |
| Nigeria | Lagos | 650 000 |
| Ghana | Tema | 342 882 |
| Liberia | Monrovia | 50 000 |
| Guinea | Conakry | 47 000 |
| Togo | Lomé | 42 240 |
| Sierra Leone | Freetown | 25 000 |
| Mauritania | Nouadhibou | 21 000 |

All cargo is worked using the ships' own cargo gear. There is covered storage of 16,500 m$^2$ and open storage of 59,000 m$^2$, with a large container stacking area with a capacity of approximately 1,000 TEUs. There is also refrigerated storage operated by fishing companies.

Port costs are fairly high and can be traced to the need for major improvements. There are berthing problems and quay congestion due to the lack of deep water berthing space, reduced channel widths, obstacles, lack of daylight operating hours, poor lighting and advance prioritizing of vessel calls. Privatization would bring in investment in port services and provide for example longer berth lengths, wider turning circles for large ships and deeper access channels alongside berths for modern ships.

*Source:* Harding et al. (2007).

The transformation of the Port of Freetown through a landlord approach will have important implications for its competitive position vis-à-vis other West African ports. No West or Central African port ranks among the top 70 ports worldwide and no large port serves as a regional hub due to poor land links, security and inefficient publicly owned operations with inadequate equipment. Most ports cannot receive ships exceeding 2,500 TEUs, even though ships of more than 6,000 TEUs are now common on international routes (box III.5). This has contributed to costly delays and congestion in ports. Nigeria's recent port reform is leading the way in major transformations that are needed in regional ports. In this context, Freetown is a small port but moving ahead with privatization would help position it well in comparison to other regional ports. It is important to target improvements in productivity and the reduction of time and cost of using the Freetown Port. If this is achieved, the port would have the potential to unload and redistribute smaller cargos destined to neighbouring ports as noted before.

To obtain the investment required to bring about the port's transformation, there are several requirements Sierra Leone must meet. There should first be good governance throughout the process. The bidding process must be clear and transparent with no corruption and a clear role for the port authority. There must also be good safety and security measures. From an operational perspective, there must be reliable document procedures (electronic and online), quality and sufficient capacity in landside connections and port infrastructure, smooth customs procedures and, for workers, continuous technical improvement through training plans (UNCTAD, 2007c).

## c. Industrial zone development

One possible avenue to develop basic infrastructure on a limited and local scale is to rely on industrial zones. Such zones can provide infrastructure services that may not be available in the country as a whole at a relatively low development cost. It is possible, for example, to allow self-generation of electricity, access to water or a link to a main transport facility. The area would thus benefit from above average facilities without necessarily solving infrastructure deficiencies at the national level. A number of countries, including in Asia, have relied on industrial zones to overcome infrastructure shortages, and perhaps also to provide

---

### Box III.5. Trends in shipping industry and port operations

About 25 of the main shipping lines (e.g. Maersk Sealand, Evergreen, P&O Nedlloyd, Haniin and Cosco) control over half the container transport capacity in world trade. Shipping alliances are also accelerating this concentration, two of which are the Great Alliance (NYK, Hapag Lloyd of Germany, the Anglo-Dutch company P&O Nedlloyd, Orient Overseas Container Lines of China and the Mediterranean Shipping Company) and the New World Alliance (Mitsui OSK Lines of Japan, APL/Neptuno Orient Lines of Malaysia and Hundai Merchant Marine of Korea), which are influential in determining trade routes and ground services.

Another trend is towards mega container vessels, which require fewer stops on the main routes. On the other hand, these vessels require increased services from feeder ships and ports with greater capacity. With the shift to the container industry, the structure and organization of terminal operations have changed towards private port terminal operating companies including stevedoring and shipping lines that are managing their container terminals as hubs and trans-shipment ports. This implies that these companies are given docking priority and guaranteed availability of equipment for use.

The provision of port-to-port logistical services by shipping lines (e.g. Maersk Logistics, Evergreen American Corporation) involves intermodal service providers and a port-to-port supply chain. This range of logistical services, which includes the consolidation of containers, documentation services, and storage and distribution, will continue to expand and improve, having a greater impact on reducing costs and enhancing efficiency.

*Source:* Gallegos (2000).

above average regulations and services (e.g. in terms of access to land, business registration or customs clearance).

Industrial zones development is an area where private foreign investment would be possible in Sierra Leone. The experience of other countries is that these zones can be developed as fully private enterprises, but in many cases, they occur under a joint venture arrangement between the public sector (providing equity in the form of land) and the private sector, which is in charge of building the infrastructure and running the zone.

The traditional, subsidy-driven free export zones popular from the 1970s through the 1990s did not work for most countries and are not likely to work for Sierra Leone (UNCTAD, 2007c).[70] Instead, a new and modern industrial zone development is needed. There has been some initiative taken to develop industrial zones such as the Guoji Industrial Zone project described in chapter I; however, the relevant legal provisions, integrated strategy and promotion plans have not materialized. The success of the industrial zone to contribute to economic growth and development crucially depends on the degree of absorption of labour, linkages with the domestic economy and consistency with investment reforms, particularly those reforms related to the privatization of port services, customs modernization and infrastructural development.

Based on Sierra Leone's comparative advantages, a case can be made for the development of a small industrial zone. Some of the advantages that investors would value in the zone relate to:
- Strategic maritime location: surrounded by flat terrain, the Port of Freetown is suitable to industrial projects requiring wide open spaces;
- Labour force: Sierra Leone has an abundance of young anglophone workers who, when matched with appropriate training programmes, could become an attractive characteristic for potential investors. FDI in the past has been motivated by low costs and labour availability; increasingly this has shifted, and quality and skills are becoming the determinants in many industries. A proper mix of low cost and high skills is now a powerful way to attract FDI in the labour-intensive industries. However, as suggested in chapter II, the proper mix will be attained through increased training programmes for workers in order to raise labour productivity (which will, at the same time, result in higher salaries);
- Supplier base: given Sierra Leone's increasing domestic market and growing mining and telecommunications sectors, the potential exists for the development of manufactures. With SLIEPA heading a strong linkages programme as proposed later in the chapter, this characteristic could evolve into a much stronger asset from an investor's perspective.

Given that Sierra Leone has no manufacturing tradition, it is not realistic to hope to attract large global exporters. Initially, the country will most likely be in a position to attract only a few investors who would focus on producing small items and basic goods to serve the increasing domestic demand. This activity would in turn provide the experience needed to serve similar market demands of regional ECOWAS countries. The focus for the zone development should therefore be on simple manufacturing and services for the local market with flexibility for other activities such as construction materials, agricultural processing and assembly work. Privileges should also apply to exports but, as argued before, initially attracting export manufacturing should not be the principal goal. Examples of the initial investment targets for the types of goods to be produced include low cost production related to processed foods, basic household items of high demand, inputs and packaging materials for agricultural products.[71] As a medium- to long-term goal, the

---

[70] Providing a tax-free environment for an unlimited period of time is excessive and attracts mostly "non-sustainable" investors that choose investment locations mainly for incentives purposes and operate as enclaves with very limited linkages with the economy.

[71] Examples of some of these products are: processed foods from grains and edible oil, fish meal, coffee, cocoa, ginger, fruit juices, wheat flour, cooking ingredients and cassava; household items such as water containers, water disinfectant products, insect repellent, mosquito nets, ice and packaging materials; inputs for processing of coffee, cocoa, palm oil and ginger; basic products for the bottle and drink industry, wooden furniture industry, artisanal fisheries (nets, wooden boat parts, motor repairing); and simple agricultural tools. Other examples include basic generic medicine drugs to treat malaria, inputs for manufacturing of plastic products, personal and household cleaning products, shoemaking and products linked to mining activities.

potential of industrial zone development would expand to take advantage of Sierra Leone's duty-free access to the growing ECOWAS markets from its strategic maritime location.

While in the short term the main goal is not to pursue export through the industrial zone, over the medium term consideration should be given to the option of combining a multi-facility zone with export promotion measures. In particular, the industrial zone development project would provide a focal point for administering, in an efficient manner, generally applicable relief schemes of indirect taxes (duty drawback and value added tax refund schemes) for the promotion of exports. This opportunity would become more viable as experience is gained through the development of an industrial zone dedicated to serving the domestic market.

In order for Sierra Leone to extract the most benefit from its location, an industrial zone should be developed adjoining the Port of Freetown through a private investment project as noted before. African investors should be the primary target for development of the zone and for future tenants. The selection of an investor to build and operate the zone should be conducted through a tender procedure. Some of the key features to be provided as part of the zone development include:

- Access to the port and local markets through proper road connections;
- Minimum operational conditions including a supply of electricity and the right to self-generating capacity, a continuous supply of water and a telecommunications network gateway to assure telephone, fax and Internet services;
- Access to a special customs procedures to expedite import/export clearances particularly for imports;
- Ability to sell self-generated power to the national grid or to have distribution and retail rights in Freetown;
- Exemption from import duties on imports such as (a) fixed assets, including equipment and machines, construction materials, transport equipment, components and parts; and (b) materials needed for zone infrastructure investment;
- Other business measures that should be implemented include competitive tax rates, no indirect taxes on exports, investment facilitation services by SLIEPA, special certification of origin to facilitate duty-free access to ECOWAS and other major global markets.

The rationale for the close proximity of the industrial zone to the port area is based on international experience and trends for waterfront development projects. In many countries, this approach is having a positive economic impact on seaport development, industrial zone planning and related land use. Developing port master plans, with regular updating, is an effective tool for port and industrial zone development and management.

The zone developer should also have the potential to be the port concessionaire. The strategic importance of this possibility is to recognize that seaports are no longer solely landing places or terminals; instead they are becoming sophisticated and integrated systems providing a full range of services for the maritime industry and for logistics activities (box III.5). They are the interface between the maritime and inland modes of transport providing multidimensional activities within the logistics chain. In this case, and assuming that the privatization of the Port of Freetown under a landlord approach has been fully approved, apart from operating the port, the company could use surrounding areas of the port to develop a multi-purpose industrial zone. In addition, the company might be able to offer value added port services including railway services and other industrial usage. For example, activities could include a stevedoring company that is also the logistical service provider, container shipping, terminal holding container and related services and manufacturing activities of the industrial zone.

### d.    Other private sector investment opportunities in infrastructure

As noted, the need for investments in infrastructure is huge. This situation requires prioritization to ensure that strategically important areas are addressed soonest. For example, to realize the potential in areas such as tourism and fisheries and to reach poverty reduction targets, there is a case for prioritizing investment promotion in the following areas where private investors would be in a position to play a useful role:

- Laboratory inspection capacity on sanitary/phytosanitary issues, including food inspection;
- Warehousing and storage buildings for agricultural products;
- Irrigation projects;
- Possible construction of a new airport or renovation of existing facilities.

Some countries in the region are considering allowing foreigners to invest in infrastructure (e.g. hydroelectric power generation) in exchange for granting mining rights. This approach is being promoted by the Chinese Development Bank (CDB) in relation to Guinea's bauxite resources. The CDB agreed to fund a $1 billion hydropower dam for rights to mine bauxite. While this may present an appealing alternative, if pursued, a cost/benefit analysis should be conducted to ensure that the benefits for the country accruing from infrastructure investment are not outweighed by the cost of relinquishing mining rights.

Investment opportunities also exist in the electricity sector. However, the reform of this sector, as in any country, is an extremely complex and lengthy process. It is therefore difficult to assess the potential for private investment in electricity in Sierra Leone as it would be determined by how reforms unfold. As noted in this report, Sierra Leone has good potential for generation of electricity with a large unmatched existing and potential demand.

## e.  Human capital

International experience shows that human capital is of strategic importance in attracting FDI and maximizing its benefits. Sierra Leone used to play an important role in education both at the country level and within the region. However, the impact of the war (it is estimated that 30 per cent of educated nationals left the country during that period) has seriously eroded the capacity to continue playing this role (box III.6). Furthermore, as is the case in many developing countries, the country suffers from a critical lack of human capital. This is explained by both the devastating impact of the war and an underinvestment in education. For

---

### Box III.6. Education in Sierra Leone

Since the nineteenth century, the country pioneered education in sub-Saharan Africa based on the British system. The Fourah Bay College (1827) was the first tertiary education institute in the region. This experience made it possible for the country to become an important training centre for teachers, doctors and administrators for West Africa in the first half of the nineteenth century.

While the tradition of an educational centre remained, it fell short of focusing on the required domains and did not reach the general population. The lack of resources devoted to tertiary education in the post-independence era as well as the war in the 1990s halted this important role.

With respect to primary and secondary education, reforms undertaken in the 1990s brought the system closer to responding social and economic needs with the objectives of increasing access, particularly to primary education, and placing more emphasis on technical and vocational education. Under current law, school attendance is required for all children for six years at primary level and three years in junior secondary level. However, shortages of schools and teachers make it difficult to reach such targets.

The 2004 Education Act abolished school fees for all children at primary school and for girls at junior secondary school in the northern and eastern regions. These provisions permitted a rapid increase in the net enrolment ratio of primary education.

*Sources:* Data from UNESCO. World Bank (2007a).

scenario 2 to materialize, it is essential to significantly increase the quality and availability of human capital and, to this end, a clear and integrated skills development strategy is required.

The strategy should be designed around four key elements: formal education, vocational training programmes, mobilization of the diaspora and conducive measures to hire foreign skilled workers when required, as highlighted above.

Wide access to quality basic education is essential as it is the building block of any attempt to move up the value chain. Experiences of host developing countries that have invested in basic education show that they have benefited from larger inflows of FDI (Miyamoto, 2003). While the Government of Sierra Leone, based on donor support, has committed to achieving compulsory basic education and the largest share of its budget goes to education, there are still more than 30 per cent of children who are not in school and completion rates at the primary level remain below 60 per cent. While quantitative gains are important, ensuring access to high quality education should also remain at the centre of the strategy. Thus, there is need to reduce teacher–pupil ratio and address the shortage of teaching and learning materials, deterioration of school buildings and furniture, low teacher incentives and motivation. Furthermore, statistics show that Sierra Leone has relatively low enrolment ratios at higher education levels. For example, gross enrolment ratios at secondary school are around 30 per cent. This is clearly insufficient to meet the more sophisticated requirements of new production processes and modern management of businesses.

In recognition of the need to increase the quality and accessibility of education, a number of initiatives by the United Nations Educational, Scientific and Cultural Organization (UNESCO) and international donors are focusing on training primary school and technical and vocational teachers.[72] Such initiatives, however, need to be complemented by policies to foster teacher retention and improve their conditions of service. This can be achieved, for instance, by providing housing, favouring transport to rural areas (including by bicycle) and reducing the delays in the payment of their salaries (it can currently take up to five months to receive the first salary upon employment) (UNESCO, 2006).

Vocational training programmes are an integral part of a development strategy for a country and they should target workers of both foreign and domestic firms. Given their knowledge of investors' requirements and closeness to activities of the labour market, the Ministry of Labour and SLIEPA must play a central role in designing these programmes. Furthermore, coordination of formal schooling and vocational education with other training policies (post-formal schooling) and programmes is necessary. This will provide students with the knowledge and skills to complement training opportunities provided in the labour market. In this regard, the role of SMEs should be fully taken into account and ways to facilitate their investment in the training of employees provided. Indeed, SMEs are typically those that would benefit most from education and training but often have limited resources for human capital formation. Furthermore, given the importance of the mining sector, some of these programmes should be designed specifically to address the needs of this sector.

## f.    Key supportive legal and institutional reforms

Building on reforms undertaken in scenario 1, additional recommendations are provided under this scenario as part of a more comprehensive reform programme. They are structured around the six areas of action proposed in chapter II. These are:

**Establishing a competitive and effective fiscal regime**. It is essential that Sierra Leone takes steps to put in place a competitive fiscal regime. In particular, the corporate income tax should be reviewed with the objective of reducing the rate to between 20 and 25 per cent for all businesses and apply a low or zero rate on export sales by agro-processing and general manufacturing industries. It is also recommended

---

[72] It is estimated that about 28,000 teachers were needed as of 2006 (UNESCO, 2006).

to eliminate provisions in sector laws (e.g. tourism) that give discretionary power to grant investment incentives. A consolidation of incentives in the Income Tax Act would be preferable. Sierra Leone should also engage in negotiations of DTTs with key partners and promote approval of the DTT ECOWAS Convention. Lastly, for projects of strategic importance, a special window dealing with tax issues should be established to provide efficient and effective services to large investors.

**Introducing supportive measures for infrastructure development**. Concerning electricity, a top priority would be to proceed with an initial rehabilitation stage of the NPA under a management contract as it is likely to be the best approach, with a longer-term view towards adding to generation capacity by contracting supply from independent power producers. This should pave the way to further reforms with private generators entering the market, an independent regulatory agency formed and preparing a future restructuring of the NPA as a limited liability company.

In the transport sector, it would be essential to ensure that a sound regulatory framework be in place to deal with initiatives from private investors to build infrastructure as highlighted above. The resolution of any legal dispute affecting investment in transport infrastructure is a necessary condition to promote investment in the sector. In the road transport sector (passenger and freight), Sierra Leone should liberalize provisions that only allow regional partners (Mano River Union, ECOWAS) to operate these transport services activities. The removal of entry restrictions for rail services in the form of joint ventures with Sierra Leoneans is also advisable. In maritime and airport services, it is recommended to eliminate the restrictions that prohibit foreign persons or firms from holding licenses for clearing or forwarding air or sea freight cargo operations, and private investors, foreign or domestic, from participating in other maritime port activities. Full implementation of the privatization of port services under a landlord approach should be a central element of the reform of this strategic sector and a reorganization of regulatory functions of port services should be undertaken with a view to creating a port authority under an independent port corporation. A new law regulating airport services would be also essential to modernize airport infrastructure and services.

**Simplifying requirements for establishing a business**. Concerning these procedures, under scenario 1, it was proposed to effectively implement the new Companies Act and ensure the efficient functioning and use of the newly created Corporate Affairs Commission. These new measures should facilitate, under scenario 2, a permanent exercise of identifying and eliminating unnecessary administrative requirements particularly in connection with business registration and licensing. In addition, SLIEPA should be tasked to facilitate the registration of business, in coordination with the Corporate Affairs Commission, to function as a single window for the collection and submission of documentation.

**Improving trade facilitation**. Sierra Leone should pursue the deepening of reforms to eliminate high costs and inefficiencies in trade transactions. It is recommended that, under the new legal framework characterized by a new Customs Law, other strategic reforms are implemented: the electronic processing and computerization of customs procedures and the effective setting up and utilization of the integrated customs information system (ASYCUDA++). To efficiently operate the new system, it would be essential to offer a full training programme to build technical capacity with a focus on customs procedures, customs information systems, technical auditing, customs warehousing, effective risk management methods and anti-smuggling procedures. Customs reform would also provide the opportunity to reorganize the management of trade activities through a mechanism to better coordinate the various agencies involved with import and export clearance.

**Facilitating the attraction of skilled workers**. To further facilitate the entry of skilled workers, and based on the efficient procedure to issue work/residence permits established under scenario 1, the government should ease labour market rigidities and define a more comprehensive package to attract workers from abroad. Mauritius provides an example of an ambitious and straightforward approach, and

Rwanda is in the process of modifying its immigration laws to facilitate the recruitment of skilled foreign workers.

**Modernizing outdated regulations**. It is essential that Sierra Leone undertakes an overall review of outdated laws to complete the modernization of the country's legal framework for investors. Although it is suggested that an overall review and inventory of laws be undertaken, efforts should give priority, in addition to the legal changes noted before, to: replace existing laws with new legislation concerning electricity, land registration rights and tourism; review and update legislation regarding mining and fisheries; and create new laws for commercial courts, competition and bankruptcy.

## g.    Judicial system

The Government of Sierra Leone recognizes the extremely poor state of the judicial system. The Justice Sector Reform Strategy and Investment Plan 2008–2010 sets out a platform for priorities and a sequence of activities to address the problems. The strategy adopts a comprehensive approach that goes beyond operational issues to include policymaking, planning and resource allocation. Limited resources have been a serious constraint to the delivery of justice and it is recognized that, realistically, the resources will remain limited in the foreseeable future. In this context, the need for effective planning, budgeting and priority setting is central.

Beyond the practical need to provide operating resources and funding for priority activities of a functioning judicial system, there are other structural issues regarding the system. The World Bank has conducted studies (Dale, 2007a and 2007b; Kane *et al.*, 2004) showing that ongoing justice reform deals primarily with formal justice systems. This implies that the customary justice systems, which are used by the majority of the population (in Sierra Leone about 85 per cent of the population fall under the jurisdiction of customary law), is largely ignored. A comprehensive approach to justice reform thus requires taking these systems into account. The reform of the dual system of common and customary laws is complex and would require careful consideration but also an assessment of how such a system interacts with central issues of functioning of market activities. A clear enforcement of contracts, property rights, arbitration and dispute resolution are few of the central issues for consideration.

## 2.    Strategic sectoral initiatives

If significant progress is achieved in addressing the key structural constraints to investment highlighted above, the FDI potential of Sierra Leone could start to genuinely unfold. The country would then end up in a much more favourable position to deploy strategic sectoral initiatives aimed at diversifying the economy, generating employment, creating wealth and reducing poverty. As estimated in section II.B, non-mining FDI inflows would have the potential to increase to as much as $250 million by 2020, assuming that the relative FDI attraction performance of Sierra Leone becomes on par with what LDCs have achieved on average in the past decade.

All sectors of the economy could undergo significant transformation if structural constraints to investment are adequately and forcefully addressed as suggested above. The services sector could undergo expansion through some additional investment in telecommunications, banking, tourism and commerce. The improved conditions and growth that would prevail in the domestic economy under scenario 2 would also provide new opportunities for small investment in basic manufacturing serving the domestic and regional markets.

A virtuous circle could also be established between higher FDI levels and additional needs for infrastructure. In such a context, FDI could make a contribution in terms of addressing some of these additional needs by providing both tax revenues for infrastructure funding and direct investments for infrastructure and human capital development. Lastly, improved growth and higher levels of FDI would be positive forces for peacebuilding through employment and training opportunities, particularly for youth.

Three main criteria were used to select sectors for strategic initiatives and to develop the related recommendations. First, targets for FDI attraction were considered in terms of compatibility with Sierra Leone's comparative advantages such as its location and ports. Second, the compatibility with development goals, particularly as they relate to poverty reduction through higher investment, productivity and employment creation was evaluated. Lastly, the domestic market was assessed from the investors' perspective in areas such as the ability to use domestic inputs, the competitiveness of labour costs and potential linkages to mining.

Defining full sectoral FDI strategies is beyond the scope of this report. Important conclusions about FDI potential in certain sectors and activities, however, can be drawn based on existing priorities and strategies. Some of the priority areas for the development of investment promotion strategies are mining, commercial agriculture, fisheries and tourism.

## a.  Mining

Even under a reformed and hospitable investment regime, FDI inflows in mining may slow in the near term. The financial crisis and the resulting deterioration in prices for base and precious metals and rough diamonds will have an impact on global mining exploration budgets, which had hit an all-time high of more than $14 billion in 2008 (Mining Intelligence, 2009). Furthermore, tight credit conditions and high capital costs are causing mining companies to reduce capital expenditures and to scale back on new mine development. Although planned investments may not materialize as quickly in the short term, in the long term, however, mining company exploration and investments will move forward.

Through a combination of the improved climate and increased FDI promotion, the sector could exceed current levels. To capitalize on the FDI in the mining sector in relation to development objectives, Sierra Leone will need to proactively foster domestic businesses along the supply chain and have in place labour force training programmes. In this climate, linkages can be established between domestic providers of goods and services for the mining industry as well as attract FDI in the manufacturing of supplies for the sector.

Although by 2009 the short-term demand and prices for minerals are uncertain, the long-term prospects of increasing global demand for these products remain robust and Sierra Leone has supply in a variety of minerals. Improved conditions, particularly in infrastructure, would allow more efficient movement of minerals from extraction sites, and the potential of mining would be increased. Under scenario 2, the planned sector reforms (box III.7) would also be carried out and would provide a much needed boost to investor confidence. The new framework, however, will require that the Ministry of Mineral Resources increase its technical capacity to supervise and properly regulate the sector. SLIEPA should also better promote investment opportunities in the sector.

As highlighted before, the improved conditions will allow SLIEPA to intensify its promotion efforts. In the mining sector in particular, the agency should embark on a campaign to promote Sierra Leone's achievements in terms of governance and contribution for infrastructure development to new mining investors. Promotion activities should include advertisement and informational articles in key international mining periodicals and journals and other publications, with a focus on business and finance in South Africa and Nigeria, as well as participation in international mining fairs and conferences in Africa. SLIEPA should also organize visits from investors in mining and work with Sierra Leonean Ambassadors to prioritize attracting investment to the sector.

Promotion activities of SLIEPA will rely on information on the current condition of the sector. This will require significant information gathering activities and coordination with the Ministry of Mining. Up-to-date geological surveys, license database, annual reporting on the sector will all be required if the proposals outlined above are to be successfully implemented.

---

**Box III.7. Upcoming institutional reform in the mining sector**

Governance problems and war have eroded the capacity of the Ministry of Mineral Resources. The ministry faces difficulties in stimulating, fostering and overseeing investment in the sector. It performs a largely administrative role and is challenged by the lack of: (i) coordination among the three divisions composing the ministry and clarity of objectives; (ii) effective central or regional monitoring and compliance structures to enforce decisions and conditions of licensing; and (iii) technical expertise.

Ongoing reforms aim at changing the functions of the ministry from administrative processing to policymaking. The focus is on:

- Reducing the transaction cost of doing business, including through improved administrative procedures for investors;
- Relying on international best practices to manage the mineral sector;
- Increasing collaboration with stakeholders and government agencies;
- Adopting open, transparent, predictable and consistent decision-making mechanisms;
- Self-financing parts of the ministry that can be commercialized or supported through licensing fees.

These reforms are key to ensuring an effective institutional framework that would be more suitable for granting licences and avoiding conflicts and legal disputes.

*Source*: Strategy and Policy Unit, Ministry of Mineral Resources.

---

## b.   Commercial agriculture

Investment in commercial agriculture will help drive growth and potential in other sectors and create more opportunities for investment. With this in mind, six areas with immediate potential for FDI in agriculture are proposed: agro-processing, commercialization services, trade finance services, farming inputs (irrigation, machinery, etc.), inspection and storage and packaging.

Coffee and cocoa export activities in Sierra Leone could be further developed with more efficient processing. As a result, initial FDI targets should be investors attracted by agro-processing activities such as washing, drying and packaging of coffee and cocoa. Current technology and efficiency in these activities is very low and the introduction of investment in these areas could become a significant contribution to income, improvement of product quality and greater competitiveness as exports. Potentially, investment could be extended also to roasting and grinding but these may only become possible after investment in basic processing and (sanitary and phytosanitary) inspection has demonstrated the overall potential for the sector.

Opportunities may also exist for commercialization services in matchmaking between existing suppliers and domestic or external demand. In general, commercial service firms would establish linkages with potential NGOs, supermarket chains and commodity trading firms or any other potential buyers. These firms would then use those linkages to search for any potential supply contracts from local producers to external purchasing firms with particular targets in coffee, palm oil, ginger and cocoa.

Technology transfer in the areas noted above should be encouraged as a transformation is needed to better exploit the country's agricultural potential. Investment would thus be instrumental in providing such technological contributions. Furthermore, specific incentives (e.g. income tax reductions, no indirect taxes applied on purchases of new machinery and technical services) should be considered to promote the use of new technologies and production methods.

Assuming that the sector would be better able to move products from production areas to domestic and foreign markets under the conditions of scenario 2, there would be the possibility of attracting investment in trade financing services. These firms would provide financing for the production or purchase of the product for sale, export financing, letters of credit, electronic payments and electronic banking, electronic funds transfer, endorsements, contractual agreements, certificate of deposit, exchange risk coverage, export credit, export credit guarantees and export credit insurance, among other services. Investment in these kinds of services would be a powerful catalyst in removing a common impediment to agricultural development.

Improved access to financing and investment in processing could conceivably lead to a significant opportunity for investment in farming inputs. For example, current investment in irrigation infrastructure, machinery, fertilizers, tree nursery and seeds is fairly low. As agricultural production becomes more commercialized, the demand for these and similar inputs will grow. An increasing shift towards commercial agriculture will also fuel demand, in particular, for phytosanitary laboratories and inspection. Private firms investing in phytosanitary laboratories, inspection and certification activities would contribute significantly to the sector's ongoing development by ensuring compliance with foreign markets' standards and, as a result, the sector could begin to participate more significantly in world markets. As a by-product of this type of investment, opportunities would also materialize in storage facilities and packaging.

When developing the commercial agriculture sector and formulating appropriate policies, consideration must be given to the role of women in this sector (box III.8). The evidence is overwhelming as to the critical role of women in agricultural production. Thus, enough emphasis cannot be placed on the importance of a

---

**Box III.8. Commercial agriculture and women**

Often overlooked, women's contribution to agriculture is substantial. Recent figures indicate that women are responsible for half of the world's food production and, in developing countries, their contribution to this sector amounts to about 60 to 80 per cent. Further, statistics show that within the agricultural sector, African women perform a very high share of the work: processing food crops and providing household water and wood fuel (90 per cent); food storage and transport from farm to village (80 per cent); hoeing and weeding (90 per cent); and harvesting and marketing (60 per cent) (Saito, 1994).

However, in spite of their crucial role, it is difficult for women to reap the full benefits of commercial agriculture as their access to inputs remains very restricted. In this regard, empirical evidence shows that equal distribution of inputs within households, such as land, seed and fertilizer, would increase agricultural productivity by up to 20 per cent (Alderman *et al.*, 1995). The disparity between women and men's access to resources is highlighted by the following examples.

*Land*: Kenyan women provided 75 per cent of agricultural labour but owned just 1 per cent of land (WEMOS, 2001). Women in Cameroon contributed similarly and owned 10 per cent of the land (Mehra and Hill Rojas, 2008).

*Implements/supplies*: In an irrigated rice project in the Gambia, less than 1 per cent of women owned a seeder, weeder or multi-purpose cultivation instrument, compared to 27, 12 and 18 per cent, respectively, of men. Research in Burkina Faso on men and women who grew the same crop on individual plots showed that most inputs, such as labour and fertilizer, went to the men's plots (Mehra and Hill Rojas, 2008).

*Financing*: An analysis of credit schemes in Kenya, Malawi, Sierra Leone, Zambia and Zimbabwe found that, overall, women had received less than 10 per cent of the credit directed to smallholders and 1 per cent of the total credit to agriculture (the same percentage as for Africa as a whole) (Mehra and Hill Rojas, 2008).

*Transportation*: Village surveys in Burkina Faso, Uganda and Zambia have found that African women move, on average, 26 metric ton-kilometres a year (especially water and wood fuel) compared with less than 7 metric ton-kilometres for men. This, combined with women's contribution to agriculture, has led to rough estimates that women contribute about two thirds of the total transport effort (World Bank, 2000).

*Sources*: FAO, World Bank and various studies cited.

---

> ## Box III.9. Sierra Leone–EU fisheries cooperation
>
> The EU Fisheries Partnership Agreement dates back to 1990; however, this agreement has not been in force since 2006. This is a consequence of an EU ban on imports of various types of fish (e.g. Atlantic big-eye tuna, blue-fin tuna and swordfish) due to health and food safety concerns that started in 2004. It was followed by an EU decision, announced in 2006, to exclude Sierra Leone from the list of countries and territories from which gastropods products such as gastropods, molluscs and fishery products were permitted. The primary cause underlying the decision is the lack of EU-approved cold storage establishments or freezer vessels and sanitary inspection capacity.
>
> In spite of the ban, there is a programme funded by the European Commission with additional contributions provided by two other members, the Netherlands and the United Kingdom, to improve Sierra Leone's future prospects as a fish exporter to the EU. The Strengthening Fishery Products Health Conditions Programme will assist the country to put in place the health and sanitary requirements of the European Commission. In addition, there is a regional project including the Gambia, Ghana, Liberia and Sierra Leone that aims at improving access to world markets for fishery products. The project focuses on strengthening health controls on exports and improving production conditions with the objective of building the capacity of inspection authorities. This includes increasing the capacity of testing laboratories and improving the sanitary practices used by the fishing industry (vessels and processing plants).
>
> *Source*: European Commission.

comprehensive policy approach – a participatory, gender-inclusive approach that clearly sets out economic, social and political initiatives aimed at empowering women. Ultimately, in order to reduce poverty and engender a flourishing, commercial agricultural sector in Sierra Leone, women must be able to have equal access and the ability to partake of the benefits.

### c.    Fisheries

The abundance of wild fish and shellfish in Sierra Leone's territorial waters makes its fishing products highly attractive as global demand for non-farmed, wild fish products is high. In order to capitalize on this comparative advantage, investment promotion in this industry should target the niche markets for wild fish products where premiums tend to be higher. The positioning of investment in fisheries should therefore be focused not on large commercial operations but on smaller scale production that would be able to capture high revenues from product quality instead of quantity. SLIEPA should play a central role in identifying these markets and potential investors.

There are important policy ramifications to attracting investment in this sector and fostering its growth. Of top priority is developing sustainable and environmentally sound catch sizes. New surveys and samplings of stock levels as well as the adoption of a regulatory framework that is consistent with the sustainability of these resources are needed to address this policy need. Of equal importance is addressing sanitary inspection and standard certification. Sierra Leone has not yet satisfied the requirements to become part of the EU's harmonized trading system, and therefore cannot export fish directly to the EU (box III.9). Sierra Leone needs to develop sanitary food inspection with sufficient laboratory and technical methods that are all certified according to international standards, particularly those of the EU as a top export destination.

Although fish products from Sierra Leone are not allowed into the EU, there are fishing vessels with self-contained processing abilities that are fishing in Sierra Leonean territorial waters and trans-shipping fish from Sierra Leone to foreign markets, including the EU. There is a major need to address this practice, which is depleting Sierra Leone's stocks in an unplanned and unsustainable manner, in particular, by putting in place an enforceable surveillance system.[73] The system would monitor commercial fishing and would control

---

[73] Basic requirements of such a system would include radars, small airplanes for monitoring and interception boats, in addition to technically qualified personnel and sufficient operational budgets.

authorized activities and drastically reduce or eliminate illegal fishing. To increase effectiveness, plans for a surveillance system should be coordinated with neighbouring Guinea and Liberia.

Investment in proper handling and cold storage facilities would also boost trade in this sector. One approach would be to promote the development of the ice-making industry, assuming sufficient electricity supply has already been achieved. Investment in fishmeal and fish oil processing in the proposed industrial park (adjacent to the port) should also be promoted.

In addition to the recommendations above, there are several important programmes and regulatory reforms for the fisheries sector where implementation has been slow or non-existent. Under scenario 2 there should be sufficient capacity to move forward with these initiatives. In particular the new Fisheries Product Regulations should be finalized, a master plan developed for fisheries addressing investment in infrastructure (e.g. storage, inspection, etc.) and the establishment of a Joint Management Authority on Fisheries with participants from the Ministries of Agriculture, Health, Natural Resources and other stakeholders representing ports, fishermen associations and SLIEPA.

## d.   Tourism

There are various efforts underway to revitalize the tourism industry in Sierra Leone, but these efforts are challenged by high operating costs and strong competition from better established West African destinations such as Benin, Côte d'Ivoire, the Gambia, Ghana and Senegal. Under scenario 2, infrastructure improvements can be expected to reduce operating costs, but competition will continue to pose a problem. To cope with this challenge in the early stages of this sector's development, the most feasible approach is an integration of Sierra Leone as part of West African tour stops. Combined with the improved conditions of scenario 2, this would trigger other investment into the sector.

Several initiatives to revitalize the sector are in the early design stage. One such initiative is being carried out by the National Tourist Board to define a strategic plan and legal reform. This could also be combined with other initiatives such as the Western Peninsula Development Project by FIAS/ World Bank (box III.10).

There are other programmes that should be given priority if the sector is to be developed further. Simplification of tourism visas and a review of fee structures should be a top priority. The United States is often cited as a target market for tourists to West Africa; however, a visa costs $131. The closest target

---

**Box III.10. The World Bank (FIAS) project for the development of the Western Peninsula**

The Western Peninsula is composed of forested mountains, crystal clear rivers and 40 km of white and golden sand beaches recognized as some of the best in West Africa. The roads to the Western Peninsula are under construction. At present, there are no public services available on the peninsula, including electricity, sewer, waste and water, implying very challenging conditions for its development. The most frequently cited barrier to developing the area is the complete lack of public infrastructure and also the absence of a land titling system.

The current development plan under consideration comprises three phases. First, the peninsula and reserve are to be declared a National Tourism Asset with a dedicated board in charge of overseeing the master plan for their development. Second, on the basis of recommendations to be proposed by the future board, the government will elaborate an action plan to build the required infrastructure. Finally, using feasibility and needs assessments along with cost analysis, conservation and community development initiatives will be implemented. It has been estimated that an investment of approximately $24–$25 million would be needed to launch a project of this nature, with additional funds to prepare the master plan, geographic information system work, environmental and coastal zone planning, and participatory planning with communities.

*Source:* FIAS (2006).

markets are the EU and the United Kingdom; however, visa fees from there average $70. Another priority is the development of a new marketing programme created with the cooperation of SLIEPA to promote Sierra Leone's new image. Lastly, a comprehensive training programme should be implemented for persons interested in working in the hospitality field.

### 3.   Implications for FDI promotion and targeting

The greatly improved investment environment prevailing under scenario 2 will only increase the importance of SLIEPA's role in investment attraction. Some of SLIEPA's primary functions would need to be expanded to include professional research and analysis, overseas promotion, policy advocacy, aftercare and image-building. ECOWAS and South Africa remain the primary targets where the promotion campaign would be intensified. Under scenario 1, promotional activities were focused primarily on image-building and more passive efforts; under scenario 2, the improved conditions would permit more ambitious and proactive FDI attraction efforts.

### a.   Research and analysis

Under scenario 2, the intensified promotion will require that SLIEPA engage in significant research and analysis. SLIEPA will need the technical capacity to identify appropriate investors according to the sectors' needs. A key task is assigning an in-house SLIEPA officer to build on existing information from the ministries and relevant sectors to identify and carry out research and analytical tasks based on an appropriate and feasible work plan. The work plan should also be used to decide on either contracting out specific additional research and analytical work, or assigning additional SLIEPA staff to do these tasks. The main initial targets of research and analysis work would focus on:

- Market intelligence related to identifying specific potential investors with the main focus on ECOWAS countries and the rest of Africa. Additional identification of potential investors from other specific countries may also become necessary;
- Developing and maintaining a database of current and potential investors;
- Identification of investment opportunities in priority sectors. This information would be critical in pursuing the identification of specific investors;
- Identification and characterization of the regional competition for FDI that Sierra Leone faces vis-à-vis ECOWAS countries. This information would be useful to target those activities that would increase Sierra Leone's competitiveness vis-à-vis regional competition;
- Targeting promotional activities to overcome the barriers to information about Sierra Leone's investment opportunities (see below);
- Producing information sheets and other written materials about industry- and sector-specific investment opportunities. The first major step in this direction came with the drafting in 2008 of A Business Guide to Sierra Leone (World Bank (FIAS) and DFID project). This publication should be updated on an annual basis;
- Producing promotional literature both online and in paper format including smaller, pamphlet-length versions of the Business Guide, as well as more specialized fact sheets or short studies aimed at specific sector audiences.

Although the promotion efforts will be less targeted outside of the region, there are passive measures which can be used to enhance investors' experiences. Many of these were addressed under scenario 1. One such area is business visa issuance. Under scenario 1, several countries were recommended for a "priority list". Under scenario 2 it is recommended that SLIEPA work with immigration on business entry visas to "fast track" (24-hour turnaround) those investors who are not from countries on the priority list. This approach integrates SLIEPA in the investor's experience at a very early stage in the process.

### b.   External promotion efforts through Sierra Leone's overseas missions

External promotion efforts should be led by the country's embassies and High Commissions with priority tasks assigned to Sierra Leone's missions to countries in the region, such as Ghana and Nigeria, and to countries of strategic importance based on priority sectors for FDI, such as Canada and Switzerland. Countries with large investment outflows or investment development programmes in Sierra Leone should also be included such as China, France, Germany, the United Kingdom and the United States, as well as the European Commission.

To undertake an effective and coordinated effort, it is recommended that an investment promotion training programme be developed for diplomats who handle investment promotion duties. The design of the training curriculum should be based on an investment training needs assessment. The training material should focus exclusively on investor targeting: promotion of target sectors and identification of specific investment projects, investors' identification and contact programmes, and image correction tasks. The course should also have a distance learning training component for future use as training programme for diplomats on investment promotion techniques.

An initial course should be held for officials in these posts with the requirement that any official posted to these missions should receive the corresponding training before the beginning of their assignment. Promotional materials should be prepared in advance of the training and made widely available in the embassies and High Commissions.

## c.    Policy advocacy

Policy advocacy should also become a central feature of SLIEPA's work under this scenario. The specific goals would be aimed at helping shape the investment climate on central problems facing FDI; promoting policies that would extract the greatest benefits from FDI, particularly in connection with the transfer of technology, human capital formation, linkages with domestic firms and employment creation; supporting policy measures that are focused on a constant effort to improve competitiveness such as the elimination of red tape and of bureaucratic burdens, the reduction of trade transaction costs, competitive taxation and the elimination of corruption.

To carry out the specific tasks of policy advocacy, a work plan should be drafted based on a four-step process: (i) problem identification and agenda setting; (ii) developing a policy remedy; (iii) consensus building; and (iv) monitoring and evaluation. The tools available for identifying policy advocacy issues should include investor surveys, aftercare services and public-private sector forums.

## d.    Aftercare and promotion of domestic linkages

As part of the more comprehensive approach of SLIEPA's work under this scenario, it is recommended that aftercare receive more emphasis. Under scenario 1, a linkages programme was recommended. In scenario 2, the development of this programme should intensify and the database of domestic suppliers, domestic demand and FDI should be expanded. Additional information should be added to the database such as national/foreigner joint ventures and additional new foreign firms that would be ready to respond on a competitive basis to the needs of foreign firms. Under scenario 2, Sierra Leone should also create its own EMPRETEC centre, which would foster the creation of mutual beneficial linkages between Sierra Leonean SMEs and foreign companies. In fact, the centre would provide training to domestic SMEs to strengthen their entrepreneurial behaviour and management skills, thus improving their supply capacity. Moreover, by increasing their competitiveness, the centre would also contribute to the progressive formalization of local SMEs, thus encouraging TNCs to use them as direct business partners. The EMPRETEC centre and SLIEPA should obviously work closely together in order to maximize linkages opportunities.

The information about SLIEPA's aftercare services for foreign investors should have a prominent place in promotional materials. This will provide a much needed assurance to foreign investors that SLIEPA facilitation services are available to foreign investors.

### e.    Image-building

Under the assumption of this scenario that the economic and investment situation in Sierra Leone has significantly improved, a more extensive image-building campaign focused on the investor community should be carried out. There should be enhanced coverage by the regional media, including the written press and television. In addition, key publications would be targeted (*Financial Times, The Economist*) to feature a general "country supplement" on Sierra Leone. Embassies, with particular emphasis in the African region, would be tasked to bridge the image gap by disseminating information and organizing targeted outreach events.

In order to fully develop an image correction campaign it is recommended that SLIEPA begin by identifying investors' current perceptions of Sierra Leone through the use of reviews of past surveys (e.g. UNIDO *Africa Foreign Investor Surveys*, World Bank *Doing Business Reports*) and by conducting new surveys. Based on this work, specific programme objectives would be defined. Once completed, these surveys would then be used to develop marketing strategies that would address the primary misconceptions investors have of Sierra Leone. The surveys will also be helpful in identifying the most cost-effective marketing mediums such as a combination of print, CD-ROMs, Internet, targeted advertising campaigns, public relations and seminars and conferences.

### 4.    Engaging fully in regional and investment development programmes

Under an ambitious scenario, Sierra Leone needs to maximize the use of existing investment programmes, particularly those related to African initiatives. It is therefore recommended that particular emphasis be placed on the programmes of Africa Union's NEPAD, ECOWAS Bank for Investment and Development, the African Development Bank (AfDB) and the China Development Bank (CDB).

NEPAD has developed an ambitious agenda for increasing investments in Africa. Furthermore, the African Peer Review Mechanism is creating more credibility under NEPAD on the potential of creating investment in Africa. By committing African governments to a high standard of economic management and transparent political processes, the mechanism will contribute to create an enabling environment for investment.

The ECOWAS Bank for Investment and Development has recently been reorganized to better address financing of ECOWAS and NEPAD projects and programmes, notably for transport, energy, telecommunications, industry, poverty alleviation, the environment and natural resources. In September 2008 a memorandum of understanding at the ECOWAS-China Forum was signed to encouraging the building of partnerships between Chinese and ECOWAS enterprises with a view to improving and enhancing their production capacity for export goods to other markets.

The AfDB continues placing priority on investment in infrastructure projects in the sectors of transport, telecommunications, power, water supply and sanitation. Its private sector lending arm also makes available direct financing to private investment projects in the form of loans, equity, quasi-equity and guarantees, as well as lines of credit to local financial institutions for on-lending to private enterprises. The AfDB does not distinguish between national and foreign ownership and some of the projects financed under the private sector programme have included foreign investors. The operation of the AfDB's private sector arm in riskier countries encourages foreign investors to enter into those frontier markets by boosting their confidence and is facilitating the use of new business approaches and financing instruments. In addition, the AfDB can also assists with FDI promotion in two areas: good governance and human resource development. Another initiative is PPPs. Arrangements include service contracts, management contract and leases to the more complex operations of BOT, BOOT (build, own, operate and transfer) and concessions.

The establishment of the China-Africa Development Fund is linked to funding from the CDB. As the main initiator of the fund, the CDB addresses issues through the Development Finance and Sino-Africa

Economic Cooperation Forum. The fund amounted to $1 billion in 2007 with the objective of eventually reaching $5 billion. The business scope of the fund deals with equity and quasi-equity investment, fund investments, fund management, investment management and consulting services. The fund will be used to support African countries' agriculture, manufacture, energy sector, transportation, telecommunications, urban infrastructure, resource exploration and the development of Chinese enterprises in Africa.

## F.  Conclusion

Given the situation prevailing in Sierra Leone and the need for substantial resources to achieve economic and social development, the government has included FDI as an integral part of its strategy to meet this goal. While in recent years, the country has benefited from higher levels of FDI inflows especially in the mining sector, it is sensible to think that it will take time for non-mining FDI to increase significantly. In this context, it is reasonable to form expectations that are in line with this reality and to focus on a long-term strategy to reach the ultimate objective of the government.

The two scenarios presented in this chapter are consistent with this vision. They are not mutually exclusive and should be seen as complementary elements of an overall strategy to stimulate investment. While the focus of the proposed strategy is mainly on FDI, each scenario is characterized by a number of recommendations that will contribute, if effectively implemented, to addressing the country's shortcomings in terms of infrastructure, human capital and regulatory framework, thereby benefiting both domestic and foreign investment. The strategy also proposes avenues to target sectors with growth potential and to provide effective FDI facilitation services.

Annex 3 summarizes the main recommendations for the two scenarios and provides guidance on implementation sequencing. For example, while all recommendations are required to meet the objectives of a given scenario, the table highlights a two-stage process for implementation.

# CHAPTER IV

# MANAGING DEVELOPMENT CHALLENGES BY ATTRACTING BENEFICIAL FDI TO SIERRA LEONE: MAIN FINDINGS AND RECOMMENDATIONS

Sierra Leone is a country of important investment opportunities, endowed with rich natural resources (including minerals, fertile land, water, fish stocks and energy), a strategic maritime location, abundant labour at relatively low cost, as well as growth potential in various sectors of the economy, including services (e.g. tourism and transport), agro-business and, as expected, mining. Since 2002, the government has made significant progress, with the support of the international community, towards achieving peace and stability and the promotion of a comprehensive reform programme. In this context, attraction of FDI has become an important element of the national development strategy.

The war in 1991–2001 had very high human cost and a devastating impact on the country's economy. In addition to the loss of thousands of lives, a large number of people became refugees or were displaced. It is estimated that about 30 per cent of the educated people left the country, further adding to the loss of human capital. The war also resulted in the destruction of an already fragile infrastructure network, leaving the supply of electricity, water, transport infrastructure and other backbone services well behind the basic needs of the population.

The experience of post-conflict countries shows that peace is often fragile unless concrete policies are in place to generate employment and improve living conditions. In this respect, the current global crisis is a particularly unwelcome development, as it negatively affects economic conditions in Sierra Leone. The deterioration of the economic situation in turn causes a threat to the peace process. In addition to decreasing commodity prices, reduced trade and investment flows and remittances, developed countries may scale down official development assistance, thereby further jeopardizing the development objectives of the country.

Against this background, this review urges the international community to continue supporting the peace and economic reform processes in Sierra Leone. Regarding the specific measures for investment, the review takes note of an open and favourable FDI regulatory regime. The country has an open regime for the entry and establishment of foreign investors. In addition, the overall protection of investors is guaranteed against expropriation. Access to dispute settlement and a free transfer of funds are also guaranteed. The international framework is, however, a bit weaker as Sierra Leone has only three BITs (China, Germany and the United Kingdom) and four DTTs (Denmark, India, Norway and the United Kingdom) signed so far, with three of them being more than 50 years old. The government policy should thus target the negotiations of BITs and DTTs with key partners as they would boost the country's FDI attractiveness.

At the specific request of the Government of Sierra Leone, the report outlines the key elements of a strategy to stimulate investment (both domestic and foreign) by tapping into international best practices. The strategy is articulated around two scenarios. Scenario 1, which is consistent with a shorter-term approach, is based on a moderate overall pace of reforms, and would result in maintaining or slightly increasing FDI inflows. Scenario 2 builds upon a longer-term and more ambitious approach, which should pave the way to significantly higher levels of FDI inflows. To fully assess the impact of the inflows on the national economy, the statistical system of data collection and analysis needs to be significantly improved. A better understanding of the role and impact of FDI would in turn enable a better formulation of the FDI attraction policy.

The overall strategy proposed in this report is anchored on six pillars: (a) tackling infrastructure deficiencies; (b) building human capital; (c) establishing a competitive and effective fiscal regime; (d) facilitating business and trade; (e) promoting and facilitating FDI; and (f) targeting investment in selected sectors. The main recommendations outlined in the report can be summarized as follows:

## A. Tackling infrastructure deficiencies

The analysis provided in the report confirms the importance of a better infrastructure if Sierra Leone is to attract and benefit from higher levels of domestic investment and FDI inflows. This is particularly true for electricity and transport infrastructure, hard hit by the war and long periods of underinvestment. The report also points to the need to develop an industrial zone to provide potential investors with adequate and efficient access to services, including electricity, water and transport links to the mainland. Furthermore, the report calls for increased involvement in the regional integration processes and programmes aimed at addressing infrastructure deficiencies, which are in turn supported by donors and development banks. While the report recognizes that it will take time to fill the infrastructure gap, it provides a number of recommendations to tackle the infrastructure challenge. While the first three recommendations are consistent with scenario 1 (shorter-term solutions), the last one would unfold in the medium term as suggested under scenario 2.

**1. Adopting laws to govern private investment in the transport and energy sectors**. The regulatory framework is neither sufficiently clear nor complete with regard to the role of, and relationship between, private and public entities in infrastructure development. A new framework is therefore required to govern, among others, partnership agreements, bidding processes, the role of other stakeholders (such as civil society), the role of independent regulators in approving and monitoring projects and competition issues. The absence of an adequate framework and institutional deficiencies has led to legal disputes, which tend to discourage potential investors from undertaking new projects.

**2. Putting in place a technical task force for energy-related issues**. As highlighted in the report, the supply of electricity in Sierra Leone is a critical problem, with only 2 per cent of households having access to it. To tackle this problem, a technical task force consistent with the Energy Sector Strategy Note of 2007 should be put in place as soon as possible to move forward the power sector reform strategy and the related action plan. The task force should also define urgently the regulatory framework governing the Special Purpose Company that will be responsible for an important hydroelectric project – Bumbuna – that is currently slowed down by its undefined relationship with the National Power Authority.

**3. Launching the development of an industrial zone**. Presently, there are very limited manufacturing activities in Sierra Leone due to many deficiencies extensively discussed in this review. While the perspective for the exports of manufacturing goods is likely to remain gloomy in the short term, there is a potential to better serve the local market by providing potential manufacturers with a location where they could have easier access to basic infrastructure. In addition to producing simple manufacturing products, the experience gained through such an initiative could pilot start a longer-term multifacility zone with export promotion features.

**4. Using regional programmes for infrastructure development**. There are many ongoing and emerging projects in West Africa to fill the infrastructure gap. These projects range from transport corridors, electricity generation and transmission to water supply and sanitation. By engaging fully in the regional integration process and in NEPAD, Sierra Leone could tap more benefits from these projects and ensure its fair share in the development of the region.

## B. Building human capital

Close to 30 per cent of educated people left the country during the war. As a result, the lack of skilled labour ranks high among the many challenges Sierra Leone faces. Thus, in spite of a large labour force and the abundance of slack labour looking for jobs, investors have difficulties finding workers who possess the right skills for the jobs they can offer. The lack of appropriate training programmes further exacerbates these problems. To address them, the report makes the following proposals:

- Establish a human capital development strategy, which should focus on formal education, vocational training, mobilization of the diaspora and measures to attract foreign skilled workers;
- Facilitate the entry of skilled workers by simplifying the procedures to issue work and residence permits and accompany this measure by an incentive package to attract workers. These measures should extend to the important community in the diaspora to incite them to return and contribute to the development of the country;
- Provide incentives to business to engage in vocational training. Formal education is a necessary but not sufficient condition, even in developed countries, for ensuring that workers have the required skills. As the economy develops, this recommendation will become increasingly important to follow up on;
- Revise, over the medium term, labour laws that foster a flexible and competitive labour market that reflects best practices in comparator or neighbouring countries.

## C. Establishing a competitive and effective fiscal regime

An attractive fiscal regime is an essential element of a package that stimulates investment as well as ensuring adequate revenue streams to finance public expenditures. In fact, whereas the government should ensure an effective fiscal regime to collect sufficient revenues, it also plays a key role in the country's ability to attract FDI. Therefore, as highlighted in the section on taxation, several measures, both general and sector-specific, should be adopted to ensure the transparency, simplicity, stability and competitiveness of the fiscal regime. In addition to the rapid introduction of the value added tax, the general measures proposed in this report also include, among others, to:

- Review the corporate income tax;
- Remove restrictions on the utilization of loss carry-forward;
- Provide equipment (computers, software for an integrated information system) and training to modernize the operations of the National Revenue Authority;
- Negotiate DTTs with key partners and approve the ECOWAS DTT.

These general measures should be accompanied by specific ones to stimulate activities in sectors recognized as important by the government. These include special fiscal conditions for the agro-processing industry, light manufacturing and mining. The measures could also take the form of additional incentives to investors in priority sectors with large-scale employment impact, or those that could self-provide infrastructure.

## D. Facilitating business and trade

Sierra Leone has made progress in terms of procedures to establish a business, as highlighted by the latest edition of the World Bank's Doing Business Report. Further changes are, however, needed to identify and eliminate remaining inefficient and unnecessary administrative requirements, particularly with respect to business registration and licensing. SLIEPA could play a role in facilitating the registration process through a single window for the collection and submission of documentation. Other strategic actions that could further improve the business environment include the effective implementation of the new Companies Act and the efficient functioning of the newly created Corporate Affairs Commission, which is in charge of harmonizing and streamlining business registration. Its role could be extended to simplifying licensing requirements, computerizing procedures and providing technical training to officials.

A number of measures could also be taken to facilitate trade, notably through improved customs procedures. As investors depend heavily on imported inputs for their activities, unnecessary delays and lengthy procedures impose high operational costs on them. While several programmes are being delivered

with support from the international community to strengthen customs operations, the Government of Sierra Leone should move forward with the:
- Approval of the new Customs Law and the finalization of the corresponding regulation to operationalize it;
- Adoption of an integrated customs information system. In this respect, Sierra Leone is in the process of launching, with the support of UNCTAD, ASYCUDA++. In addition to facilitating the processing of import and export information, such a system will also improve customs declaration, risk management, revenue collection and statistical reporting. It will also allow for the elimination of the costly PSI;
- Implementation of a training programme to build the capacity of customs officials.

Another area where the IPR has highlighted significant problems for investors, both domestic and foreign, is land tenure. In Sierra Leone, as in many African countries, there is a dual system of land tenure. The two systems are governed by different laws, making this aspect of investment decisions unclear and difficult. While the reform of land tenure is a complex and long-term endeavour, it is urgent, in the short run, to improve access to secure land right titles and conditions for market transactions.

Finally, an important area of work is the modernization of laws. Due to the war and a lack of resources prior to it, Sierra Leone is left with numerous outdated laws, some of which date back to the colonial era. Several laws have already been reconsidered since the end of the conflict. However, much more remains to be done. While this is going to be done over a long period of time, priority should be given to laws related to sectors that have been identified as potential sources of growth, such as mining, fisheries and tourism.

## E. Promoting and facilitating FDI

The consequences of the war have also had an impact on the image of Sierra Leone vis-à-vis foreign investors. After close to a decade of peace, it still remains challenging for them to picture the country as a destination for FDI. In this context, it is critical for SLIEPA to offer efficient facilitation services and help project a different image. SLIEPA's services could include:
- **Facilitation services** SLIEPA should ensure that existing and potential investors have easy access to all information needed throughout their project exploration and realization. Currently, this is not the case. Facilitation services should also include a regularly updated website containing all the necessary documents and laws. Enhancing SLIEPA's capacity to track investors is also desirable. In addition to being used as a source of statistics related to foreign investment, such a system would help the agency to better understand investors' needs and requirements;
- **Aftercare services** The resources, especially in the short run, may not be available to provide an extensive aftercare programme. However, SLIEPA could consider implementing a programme to foster linkages between foreign-owned firms and local suppliers of goods and services. In addition to fostering the localization of foreign investors and their reinvestment, such a programme would stimulate domestic economic activity while reducing the informal sector, thereby enhancing the beneficial impact of FDI. For example, Sierra Leone could benefit from training programmes delivered by EMPRETEC centres located in the subregion (Ghana and Nigeria);
- **Image-building.** As highlighted in the report, the image of Sierra Leone as a peaceful and stable country needs to be promoted, including with a well-designed and marketed Internet portal. Furthermore, since Sierra Leone will likely not attract large investors outside the mining sector in the short run, it is recommended, as a first stage, to launch a limited programme of investor targeting that will focus primarily on ECOWAS.

In the longer run, SLIEPA could develop as a full-fledged agency providing a wider range of services, including research and analysis, extensive promotional campaigns, aftercare and policy advocacy. Sierra Leone could also, in the longer term, create its own EMPRETEC centre, which would work closely with

SLIEPA in view of enhancing the development of SMEs and promoting their linkages with transnational corporations.

## F. Targeting investment in selected sectors

Sierra Leone has good investment potential in different economic activities. Short-term actions should primarily focus on the mining sector, which has traditionally attracted FDI. Longer-term actions should focus on activities, such as commercial agriculture, fisheries and tourism, that present a solid potential for attracting foreign investment and should be supported. In this regard, the report proposes the following:

- **Mining**. The sector will continue to play a leading role in attracting FDI to Sierra Leone. For the country to get an increased share of world FDI in the sector, the government should review certain taxes and levies with a view to ensuring a competitive fiscal treatment for investors while meeting long-term domestic revenue needs. At the same time, the government should also avoid individual deals with investors that include long-term tax holidays or reduced royalty payments, as they are unnecessary to attract investment and constitute a great loss of revenue. There is also a need to clarify the mandate of the Ministry of Mineral Resources as well as reform and strengthen the institution to enable it to fulfil its mandate. These measures should be accompanied by intensified promotion efforts on the part of SLIEPA;

- **Commercial agriculture.** While the potential of the sector is likely to unfold in the medium-to-long term, some investment could materialize more rapidly through targeting campaigns. Potential has been recognized in terms of coffee, cocoa, palm oil and ginger exports, and for a few other basic or processed products. Increased prospects for the production of these goods should in turn generate additional investments in irrigation, machinery, fertilizers, tree nursery and seeds. To fully tap the benefits of the sector, there will be a need to establish phytosanitary inspection and certification capacities;

- **Fisheries**. The coast of Sierra Leone is well known for its abundant wild fish and shellfish. To capitalize on this competitive advantage, investment promotion and sector plans for this industry should target the niche markets for wild fish products where premiums tend to be higher. SLIEPA should play a central role in identifying these markets and potential investors. At the same time, there is also a need to promote the adoption of a regulatory framework that is consistent with the sustainability of these resources. It is also essential to negotiate with the EU agreements that would re-establish the possibility for exports to that market. This notably includes the development of safety requirements for food processing and facilities for sanitary food inspection and certification;

- **Tourism**. Various efforts are being made to revitalize the tourism industry, but these have been mostly unsuccessful so far due to high operating costs and strong regional competition. By finalizing the strategic plan for the sector and initiating legal and institutional reforms, the government could pave the way for the development of tourism. Moving forward with pilot projects such as the Western Peninsula Development Project of the World Bank should play a catalytic role for the development of the whole sector. In this regard, a simplification of the process to obtain tourism visas and a review of the fee structure is desirable. To cope with regional competition and trigger new investments, it is recommended to integrate Sierra Leone into a West African tour as one of the stops. Finally, a marketing programme initiated with the assistance of SLIEPA to promote Sierra Leone's image should be put in place, as well as a training programme for potential workers in the sector.

## G. Conclusion

Moving the development agenda forward in Sierra Leone is a long-term process. This report has presented concrete policy recommendations to reach such an objective through the contribution of increased FDI inflows. While a solid commitment of the government is essential, it needs to be complemented by the involvement of the international community. In this context, UNCTAD can also take part in the process and provide the Government of Sierra Leone with assistance in a number of areas, including FDI promotion, FDI statistics, human capacity-building, drafting of laws and treaties, and improving access to – and dissemination of – information.

# ANNEXES

## Annex 1. Key investment-related reforms adopted since 2000[74]

| Issue | Law | Year |
|---|---|---|
| Mining | Mines and Mineral Act | 2009 |
| Company law | Companies Act | 2009 |
| Businesses | Bankruptcy Act | 2009 |
| Financial services | Payment Systems Act | 2009 |
| Financial services | Home Mortgage Finance Act | 2009 |
| Taxation | Good and Services Tax Act | 2009 |
| Telecommunications | Telecommunications (Amendment) Act | 2009 |
| Corruption | Anti-corruption Act | 2008 |
| Investment | Investment and Export Promotion Agency Act | 2007 |
| Financial services | Financial Services (stock exchanges) (Amendment) Act | 2007 |
| Telecommunications | Telecommunications (Amendments) Act | 2006/2007 |
| Maritime transport | Maritime Administration (Amendment) Act | 2007 |
| Businesses | General Law (Business Start-up) (Amendment) Act | 2007 |
| Firm registration | Registration of Business Act | 2007 |
| Electricity | National Power Authority (Amendment) Act | 2006 |
| Money laundering | Anti-Money Laundering Act | 2005 |
| Telecommunications | External Telecommunications Tax Act (amended) | 2004 |
| Mining | Mines and Minerals (Amendment) Act | 2004 |
| Investment | Investment Promotion Act | 2004 |
| Public procurement | Public Procurement Act | 2004 |
| Local government | Local Government Act | 2004 |
| Road transportation | Road Transport Authority (Amendment) Act | 2003 |
| Merchant shipping | Merchant Shipping Act | 2003 |
| Tax administration | National Revenue Authority Act | 2002 |
| Privatization | National Commission for Privatization Act | 2002 |
| Financial services | Other Financial Services Act | 2001 |
| Petroleum | Petroleum Exploration and Production Act | 2001 |
| Central banking | Bank of Sierra Leone Act | 2000 |
| Banking | Banking Act | 2000 |
| Insurance | Insurance Act | 2000 |
| Corruption | Anti-corruption Act | 2000 |
| **Draft bills (as of 2008)** | | |
| Land | Commercial Use of Land Act | 2008 |
| Consumer Protection | Consumer Protection Act | 2008 |

[74] Some laws can be consulted at http://www.sierra-leone.org/laws.html.

| Draft bills (as of 2008) | | |
|---|---|---|
| Estates | Devolution of Estates Act | 2008 |
| Partnership | Partnership Act | 2008 |
| Diamond processing | Diamond Cutting and Polishing Act | 2008 |
| Diamond trade | Import and Export of Rough Diamonds Act | 2008 |
| Local courts | Local Courts Act | 2008 |
| **Legislation under preparation/ongoing review as of 2008** | | |
| Customs | Customs Law | Ongoing |
| Law of evidence | Law of Evidence | Ongoing |
| Investment incentive | Annex, Investment Promotion (still under discussion) | Ongoing |
| Arbitration | Arbitration Act | Ongoing |
| Law officers | Law Officers Act | Ongoing |
| Courts | Courts Act | Ongoing |
| Dispute resolution | Alternative Dispute Resolution | Ongoing |
| Electricity | National Power Authority (NPA) Act (1982) | Ongoing |
| Government | Public Service Act | Ongoing |

*Source*: UNCTAD analysis based on data from http://www.sierra-leone.org/laws.html and the Law Reform Commission.

## Annex 2. Methodology of international tax comparisons

The *Comparative Taxation Survey* compares taxation on investment in several sectors in Sierra Leone with taxation in other selected countries – neighbours and countries elsewhere that have succeeded in attracting FDI to the sectors concerned. These comparisons enable Sierra Leone to assess the competitiveness of its taxation.

Corporate taxation affects the cost of investment and its profitability, and thus the return on investment. This impact is not just a question of looking at the headline rate of tax on profits. The tax burden on the investor depends on a number of factors and their interaction, including allowed expenses, rates of capital allowances (tax depreciation), the availability of tax credits, investment allowances and tax holidays, the loss carry-forward provisions and the taxation of dividends, among other things.

Comparative tax modelling is a method of taking into account the most important of these variables in the fiscal regime in a manner that facilitates comparison between countries. The tax variables included in the analysis are:
- Corporate income tax;
- Tax rates including tax holidays, if any;
- Loss carry-forward provisions;
- Capital allowances, investment allowances and investment credits;
- Tax on dividends;
- Customs import duties and excise duties on business inputs.

Sales tax is not considered in the analysis because it is to be replaced by VAT. In any event, a correctly administered VAT falls on the consumer and is not a tax burden on business.

Financial models of project investment and financing, revenues and expenses are utilized for a hypothetical business in each sector. These are based on typical costs and revenues experienced in such businesses in a developing economy. The business models cover a selected business within each sector.

The fiscal regime in Sierra Leone for each sector is applied to the standard business model for each sector over 10 years beginning with the initial investment. The financial models calculate net cash flow to the investor assuming that the company pays out all residual profits after tax (100 per cent dividend pay out) and that the investor gains the residual value of the company, which is sold after 10 years for an amount equal to its balance sheet value.

The impact of the fiscal regime is presented as the present value of tax (PV tax). PV tax is the total of taxes and duties collected by the government over the 10 years as a percentage of the project cash flow pre-tax and post-finance where both cash flows are discounted to a present value at a rate of 10 per cent per annum. PV tax thus measures how much of investors' potential project return is taken by the government in taxes and duties. The higher the PV tax, the more the fiscal regime burdens investors and reduces the incentive to invest.

For the simulation of the tax model, different incentives programmes are used. Agriculture: In Ghana, I1 is for programmes in farming and I2 in agro-processing. In Sierra Leone, I1 is for programmes related to tree crops. In Thailand, I1 is for agricultural incentives including food processing and biotechnology. Fisheries: In Ghana, I1 is for fish processing into edible canned or other packaged products, and in Viet Nam, I1 is for offshore fishing, vessel and equipment upgrading. Manufacturing: In The Gambia, I1 is for assembling and packaging, processing, foundry and forging, light pharmaceuticals. In Ghana, I1 is for businesses outside Accra/Tema in regional capitals and I2 is for programmes elsewhere. In Thailand, I1 is for activities in 58 provinces and I2 for projects in industrial estates or zones. In Viet Nam, I1 is for investments in industrial parks and I2 for investments in especially difficult socio-economic regions. Tourism: In the Gambia, II is for hotel development, hotel upgrading, cultural tourism, upcountry tourism and eco-tourism. In Ghana, II is for building properties for star-rated hotels, tourist villages and tourist attractions. In Sierra Leone, II relates to plant and equipment acquisition, and I2 to construction activities. In Thailand, II is for promotion services, hotels, lodging, health care and for projects in Zone I (the six central provinces), and I2 is a variation of II for Zone 2.

## Annex 3. Sequencing recommendations to implement the FDI strategy

| Sequencing<br>Areas of action | SCENARIO 1 | | SCENARIO 2 | |
|---|---|---|---|---|
| | **Stage 1** | **Stage 2** | **Stage 1** | **Stage 2** |
| **1. Tackling infrastructure deficiencies – electricity, transport, industrial zone** | Draft laws to govern the private sector's involvement in the transport and energy sectors.<br><br>Allow investment in selected infrastructure to qualify for tax relief on unrelated income of the investor. | Resolve legal disputes related to investment in transport infrastructure.<br><br>Put in place a Technical Task Force (based on the Energy Sector Strategy Note of 2007) to:<br>• Finalize the power sector reform strategy and action plan;<br>• Define the regulatory governing framework of the "Special Purpose Company".<br><br>Liquidate the SNA to improve investment prospects in airport services.<br><br>Identify institutional responsibility to develop an industrial zone based on international best practices.<br><br>Start identifying potential investors to develop the industrial zone. | Implement a rehabilitation stage of the NPA under a management contract.<br><br>Lift the restrictions on operators from Mano River Union and ECOWAS for transport services (passenger and freight).<br><br>Remove entry restrictions (joint ventures with Sierra Leoneans) for rail services.<br><br>Eliminate entry restrictions for clearing or forwarding air or sea freight cargo operations and allow private investors, foreign or domestic, to participate in other port activities.<br><br>Implement full privatization of port services under a landlord approach.<br><br>Reorganize regulations on port services to create a port authority under an independent port corporation.<br><br>Undertake a comprehensive assessment of electricity needs: (i) existing and potential domestic demand, geographical requirements; (ii) actual and potential demand from neighbouring countries.<br><br>Define human resource requirements for the electricity sector and design training plans to build technical and managerial capacity.<br><br>Make use of regional programmes to complement efforts in the area of infrastructure with particular emphasis on those of AfDB, CDB, ECOWAS, NEPAD and the World Bank.<br><br>Implement articles 32 and 33 of the ECOWAS Revised Treaty to:<br>• Integrate railway networks with neighbouring countries to maximize transport to hinterland areas and use of the Port of Freetown; | Prepare the restructuring of the NPA as a limited liability company and define the characteristics of a new regulatory body for the electricity sector.<br><br>Add to electricity generation capacity by contracting supply from independent power producers.<br><br>Make progress towards the interconnection of the electricity grid with neighbouring countries (West Africa Power Pool).<br><br>Approve a new law regulating airport services to modernize airport infrastructure and services.<br><br>Build a new airport or renovate existing facilities.<br><br>Target regional investors to produce, in the industrial zone, basic manufacturing goods for the domestic market.<br><br>Expand the industrial zone to a multifacility zone with export promotion measures.<br><br>Target private investors with the potential to develop:<br>• Laboratory capacity for sanitary and phytosanitary inspection, including food inspection;<br>• Warehousing and storage buildings for agricultural products;<br>• Irrigation projects. |

| Sequencing | SCENARIO 1 | | SCENARIO 2 | |
|---|---|---|---|---|
| Areas of action | Stage 1 | Stage 2 | Stage 1 | Stage 2 |
| **1. Tackling infrastructure deficiencies – electricity, transport, industrial zone (continued)** | | | • Formulate a programme to improve coastal shipping services and inter-State inland waterways<br><br>• Develop a regional air transport services programme.<br><br>Undertake an assessment of transport connectivity (road, rail and airport) with the Port of Freetown. Based on results, design and implement a programme to address shortcomings.<br><br>Undertake an assessment of basic transport services with particular emphasis on rural areas. Based on results, draw a strategy to upgrade services.<br><br>Prepare legal bases for the development of the industrial zone.<br><br>Coordinate the plan for the industrial zone with reforms related to electricity and transport infrastructure, including the port, land, customs procedures and labour regulations. | |
| **2. Building human capital** | | Initiate the preparation of a human capital development strategy that incorporates short-, medium- and long-term actions. Identify linkages with labour market reforms.<br><br>Initiate a revision of laws regulating labour to modernize their provisions and create a competitive labour market that reflects best practices in comparator or neighbouring countries.<br><br>Introduce derogation for labour market test requirements for large strategic investment projects. | Approve and implement the human capital development strategy that incorporates measures related to formal education, vocational training programmes, mobilization of the diaspora and hiring of foreign skilled workers.<br><br>Approve changes to labour laws.<br><br>Define a package to attract foreign skilled workers based on priority sectors and best practices in neighbouring countries. | Design incentives for firms to engage in vocational training and involve SLIEPA in the design of the programmes to address investors' needs. |

| Sequencing Areas of action | SCENARIO 1 | | SCENARIO 2 | |
|---|---|---|---|---|
| | **Stage 1** | **Stage 2** | **Stage 1** | **Stage 2** |
| **2. Building human capital (continued)** | | Review the criteria and process to allocate work permits to foreigners: <br>• Unify the residence and work permits; <br>• Give work authorization to dependents under certain conditions. <br><br>Eliminate the requirement that applications for work permit be submitted six months in advance and limit processing time to a maximum of one month. <br><br>Designate a centralized and unique unit to collect applications, approve and issue work/residency permits. <br><br>Make publicly available the criteria guiding the allocation of permits. <br><br>Introduce a Diaspora Attraction Programme to attract required skills. | | |
| **3. Establishing a competitive and effective fiscal regime** | Introduce the value added tax. <br>Remove restrictions on the utilization of loss carry-forward. <br>For the advance tax payments: <br>• Eliminate the 3 per cent charge on CIF imports that exists as advance tax payment; <br>• Limit advance turnover tax payment only in reference to taxes paid from a previous year. <br>Apply the same income tax rate to resident and non-resident small business owners. | Reduce and harmonize to between 5 and 10 per cent all withholding taxes on payments to service contractors, royalties, interests and dividends. <br>Clarify provisions concerning minimum chargeable business income tax. <br>Equip the NRA with an integrated information system and ensure that its main functions are computerized. <br>Ensure that VAT tax reimbursements and duty drawback run under efficient electronic systems. | Corporate income tax: <br>• Review rate; <br>• Set a low or zero rate on export sales by agro-processing and general manufacturing industries. <br>To optimize the impact of the tax reductions, implement them together with the simplification/consolidation of other taxes and with the introduction of facilitation services related to tax compliance. <br>Set a special NRA window to deal with tax administrative issues for projects of strategic importance. | Incentives: <br>• Consolidate incentives in the Income Tax Act; <br>• Eliminate provisions in sector laws giving discretionary power to grant investment incentives. <br>Introduce universally available and easily administered measures to promote specific outcomes (e.g. additional deductions for large-scale employment) and to address difficulties (e.g. investment allowances for self-provision of utilities and infrastructure). <br>Double Taxation Agreements: <br>• Negotiate DTTs with key partners; <br>• Promote approval of the DTT ECOWAS Convention. |

| Sequencing<br><br>Areas of action | SCENARIO 1 | | SCENARIO 2 | |
|---|---|---|---|---|
| | Stage 1 | Stage 2 | Stage 1 | Stage 2 |
| **4. Facilitating business and trade** | Effectively implement the new Companies Act. Based on new provisions of the Act, put in place a modern and clear regulatory framework for registry and authorization to operate businesses.<br><br>Approve the new Customs Law, which includes the WTO Agreement on Customs Valuation.<br><br>Draw up a plan to coordinate customs reforms with other reforms concerning port and trade procedures to maximize the benefits of customs reforms. Specific targets for coordination should include infrastructure improvements, customs and port law enforcement, and accounting and auditing procedures. | Give the necessary means and tools to the Corporate Affairs Commission, so that it can effectively:<br>• Harmonize and streamline registration responsibilities in coordination with the Registrar General;<br>• Simplify business registration requirements;<br>• Streamline licensing requirements;<br>• Computerize procedures for business registration and provide technical training to officials in charge.<br><br>Finalize the corresponding customs regulations to operationalize the new law.<br>Eliminate the use of PSI procedures, reference values, costly deposit payment requirements and bank guarantees for the granting of clearance permits.<br>Adopt a recent version of the Harmonized Commodity Description and Coding System of Tariff Nomenclature.<br>Create legal bases for a WTO-consistent duty drawback scheme.<br>Guarantee national treatment of FDI by formalizing it in the Investment Promotion Act. Eliminate partnership requirements for investment in services activities.<br>Review and amend specific laws dealing with foreign exchange transactions to ensure consistency between the Bank of Sierra Leone Act and the Investment Promotion Acts.<br>Reform the legal provisions for the registration of land titles and codify the resulting new legal framework for land property rights. Reform the institutional bases for cadastral issues. | Task SLIEPA to facilitate the registration of business, in coordination with the Corporate Affairs Commission through a single window for collection and submission of documentation.<br><br>Implement and effectively use the electronic processing and computerization of customs procedures and the setting up of the integrated customs information system (UNCTAD's ASYCUDA++).<br><br>Implement a training programme to build technical capacity with a focus on: customs procedures; customs information systems; technical auditing; customs warehousing; effective risk management methods; and anti-smuggling procedures.<br><br>Adopt a risk management approach for customs inspection.<br><br>Review and update legislation regarding mining and fisheries.<br><br>Replace existing laws with new legislation for electricity, land registration rights and tourism.<br><br>Prepare new laws for commercial courts, competition and bankruptcy. | Reorganize the management of trade activities through a coordinated mechanism of agencies involved with import and export clearance.<br><br>Review and update legislation regarding intellectual property rights.<br><br>Undertake a review of remaining outdated laws to complete the modernization of the country's legal framework for investors.<br><br>Make operational a commercial court. |

| Sequencing | SCENARIO 1 | | SCENARIO 2 | |
| --- | --- | --- | --- | --- |
| **Areas of action** | **Stage 1** | **Stage 2** | **Stage 1** | **Stage 2** |
| **4. Facilitating business and trade (continued)** | | Draft clear and complete procedures for access to land (for freehold and customary systems) with guidelines and information centres in Freetown and key locations in the provinces. Complete the privatization of Sierra Leone National Shipping Company. | | |
| **5. Promoting and facilitating FDI** | Provide FDI facilitation services with priority activities on: <br>• Putting in place a portal to facilitate access to information; <br>• Creating and maintaining an investor tracking database; <br>• Establishing communication facilities at SLIEPA for use by foreign investors; <br>• Reforming visa requirements to ease entry conditions for potential investors; <br>• Creating and maintaining a priority list of countries that would be exempt from the entry visa requirement; <br>• Simplifying the fee structure and reducing the fees for visas. <br><br>Focus on targeting West African investors in FDI attraction campaigns. | Aftercare services: <br>• Foster linkages between FDI and domestic suppliers through SLIEPA's list of matching firms; <br>• Support SMEs' development through participation in training programmes by EMPRETEC centres in the region; <br>• Establish an Investment Promotion Committee. <br>Promotion: <br>• Initiate a regional marketing campaign to start an image correction process; <br>• Use the country's embassies to channel the messages of the campaign; <br>• Implement a training programme for diplomats with responsibilities for investment promotion. <br>Prepare a consistent and "state-of-the art" investment treaty model to negotiate future BITs. | Implement SLIEPA research and analysis work with focus on: <br>• Market intelligence to identify potential investors with focus on ECOWAS; <br>• Developing and maintaining a database of current and potential foreign investors; <br>• Identification of investment opportunities in priority sectors; <br>• Producing information sheets and other written materials about industry- and sector-specific investment opportunities; <br>• Updating on annual basis the Business Guide to Sierra Leone (World Bank (FIAS) and DFID project); <br>• Producing promotional documentation both online and in paper format. <br>Identify investors' perceptions of Sierra Leone to define specific image programme objectives. <br>Create an EMPRETEC centre to enhance local SMEs' supply capacity and foster linkages with foreign affiliates. | Implement an extensive investment promotion campaign with enhanced coverage by regional media and with glossy publications. |

| Sequencing<br><br>Areas of action | SCENARIO 1 | | SCENARIO 2 | |
|---|---|---|---|---|
| | Stage 1 | Stage 2 | Stage 1 | Stage 2 |
| **6. Targeting sectors** | | | | |
| **1. Mining** | Implement a more competitive income tax rate in conjunction with a review of other levies (withholding taxes, royalty rates, the various other levies and local development funds). The total of these various taxes should be reviewed to better position the sector. | Implement institutional reforms at the Ministry of Mines and Energy. Complete the privatization of Mining and General Services Limited (MAGS). Intensify SLIEPA promotion efforts for the sector. | Based on a new fiscal regime for the mining sector, create transparency provisions to enforce and make public any tax treatment for mining projects. Implement SLIEPA programme of linkages between domestic suppliers and mining firms. | Implement a new attraction programme for FDI in mining through SLIEPA targeted campaigns of image-building and sector opportunities. |
| **2. Commercial agriculture** | | Target new investment in irrigation infrastructure, machinery, fertilizers, tree nursery and seeds. | Prepare a promotion campaign for investment related to commercialization services, trade finance, farming inputs, inspection and storage/packaging of priority products (coffee, cacao, palm oil, ginger). Implement phytosanitary inspection and certification infrastructure to provide standard certification for targeted products. Develop new information material for investment opportunities in the sector. | Develop SLIEPA services to identify matchmaking between existing suppliers and domestic or external demand in the form of purchasing contracts. Target further processing activities in connection with roasting and grinding of coffee. |
| **3. Fisheries** | | Continue negotiations with the EU to identify priority actions to re-establish export authorization to its member States. | Define a new sector approach to promote investment based on small-scale production destined to niche markets of natural/wild fish. Put in place a well-funded surveillance system to control illegal fishing. Promote investment in cold storage facilities and food safety process methods. | Implement new Fisheries Product Regulations. Prepare a master plan for fisheries addressing infrastructure (e.g. storage, inspection) and the establishment of a Joint Management Authority on Fisheries with participants from the Ministries of Agriculture, Health, Natural Resources and other stakeholders representing ports, fishermen associations and SLIEPA. |
| **4. Tourism** | | | Finalize and implement the strategic plan for the sector. Identify new promotional priorities. Integrate tourism within new image-building campaigns. Introduce training programmes for service providers in this sector. | Identify specific SLIEPA targets for FDI sources in tourism. Promote the development of Sierra Leone within West African regional tours. Simplify tourism visas and review the fee structures. |

# REFERENCES

Abella M (2006). Global competition for skilled workers. In: Kuptsch C and Pang Eng Fong, eds. *Competing for Global Talent*. International Labour Organization.

Adam Smith Institute (2007). *Modelling the Economic Potential of Mining in Sierra Leone*. Freetown.

Alderman H *et al.* (1995). Gender differentials in farm productivity: implications for household efficiency and agricultural policy. In: Timmer CP, ed. *Food Policy: Getting Agriculture Moving*.

African Minerals Limited (2008). Key engineering project updates. RNS Number: 8567Z. Freetown.

Bangura Z (2007). Prospects for Sierra Leone. Chatham House Speech. London. 29 November.

Barbour P (2005). *An Assessment of South Africa's Investment Incentive Regime*. London, Overseas Development Institute.

CEMMATS Group (2004). *The Energy Policy for Sierra Leone*. Addis Ababa, UNECA.

Central Bank of Sierra Leone (2007). *Balance of Payments 2004–2006 Update*. Freetown.

Central Bank of Sierra Leone (2008). *Annual Report*. Freetown.

Collier P (2006). *Economic Causes of Civil Conflict and their Implications for Policy*. Department of Economics, University of Oxford.

Collier P *et al.* (2006). Post-conflict risks. Working Paper/2006-12. Centre for Study of African Economies, Department of Economics, University of Oxford.

Dale P (2007a). Access to justice in Sierra Leone: A review of the literature. *World Bank's Justice for the Poor Programme*.

Dale P (2007b). Barriers to justice in Sierra Leone. *World Bank's Justice for the Poor Programme*. 1 (4).

Embassy of the People's Republic of China in Sierra Leone (2004). The survey of Sino-Sierra Leone mutual beneficial cooperation. http://sl2.mofcom.gov.cn/ aarticle/bilateralcooperation/inbrief/200412/20041200008095.html.

FIAS (2006). *Competitiveness and Corporate Social Responsibility in Sierra Leone: Industry Solutions for Tourism and Mining*. Washington DC.

*Financial Times* (2008). Africa's thirst for local brew. January 9.

Gal M (2003). *Competition Policy in Small Market Economies*. Harvard University Press.

Gallegos C (2000). Trends in maritime transport and port development in the context of world trade. The Inter-American Committee on Ports, Second Executive Meeting. Barbados.

Government of Sierra Leone (2007). *Poverty Reduction Strategy: Progress Report 2005–2007*. Freetown.

Harding A *et al.* (2007). Port and maritime transport challenges in West and Central Africa. Sub-Saharan Africa Transport Policy Programme working paper 84. World Bank.

Hirsch J (2001). *Sierra Leone: Diamonds and the Struggle for Democracy*. Boulder.

Hooge L (2008). *Case Study of Sierra Leone*. Addis Ababa, International Study Group on Africa Mining Regimes, Natural Resources Canada.

Horwath Consulting (1990). *Sierra Leone Indicative Tourism Development Strategy*. Freetown.

IMF (2008a). Debt Relief under the Heavily Indebted Poor Countries (HIPC) Initiative: A Factsheet. Washington DC.

IMF (2008b). *Second Poverty Reduction Strategy (PRSP II): The Republic of Sierra Leone – An Agenda for Change (2008-2012)*.

ITU (2007). *World Telecommunication Indicators*. Geneva, ITU.

Kane M *et al.* (2004). *Sierra Leone: Legal and Judicial Sector Assessment*. World Bank.

Kirkpatrick C *et al.* (2006). Foreign direct investment in infrastructure in developing countries: does regulation make a difference? *Transnational Corporations*. 15 (1).

Koidu Holdings (2008). Koidu kimberlite project history. http://www.koiduholdings.com/mining_koidu_project_history.html

McEwen D and Siaffa D (2005). Tourism development in Sierra Leone. Diagnostic Trade Integration Study. Integrated Framework for Trade-Related Technical Assistance to the Least Developed Countries. Freetown.

Mehra R and Hill Rojas M (2008). *Women, Food Security and Agriculture in a Global Marketplace*. International Centre for Research on Women.

Mining Intelligence Series (2009). Executive summary.

Ministry of Energy and Power (2007). Update on the current activities of the Ministry.

Miyamoto K (2003). Human capital formation and FDI in developing countries. Working paper 211. OECD Development Centre.

Ministry of Transport and Aviation (2007). Transport sector strategy. Presented at the DEPAC Meeting. Freetown. 29 March.

NCP (2006). *Progress Report on the Privatization Process*. Freetown.

NEPAD (2005). *Support to NEPAD-CAADP Implementation. Volume II of IV: Bankable Investment Project Profile- Sustainable Land and Water Resources Development*. Addis Ababa, NEPAD.

OECD (2003). *Checklist for Foreign Direct Investment Incentive Policies*. Paris, OECD.

PAC (2004). *Diamond Industry Annual Review: Sierra Leone*. Ottawa.

PWC (2007). *Technical Assistance to the National Commission for Privatization, Sierra Leone Inception Report.*

Saito KA (1994). Raising the productivity of women farmers in sub-Saharan Africa. World Bank Discussion Paper no. 230. Washington DC.

Smillie *et al.* (2000). *The Heart of the Matter: Sierra Leone Diamonds and Human Security*. Ottawa, PAC.

Stellenbosch University (2005). China's interest and activity in Africa's construction and infrastructure sectors. Paper prepared for DFID China. Centre for Chinese Studies. Stellenbosch.

Thomson B (2007). *Sierra Leone: Reform or Relapse? Conflict and Governance Reform: A Chatham House Report*. Chatham House, the Royal Institute of International Affairs.

TRG (2008). Company Presentation: operations at SRL. Freetown.

United Nations (2007). World Population Prospects Database. New York.

United Nations (2008). UNdata Key Global Indicators. New York.

UNCTAD (2004). *Investment Policy Review of Sri Lanka*. United Nations publication. UNCTAD/ITE/IPC/2003/8. New and Geneva.

UNCTAD (2007a). *Investment Policy Review of Rwanda*. United Nations publication. UNCTAD/ITE/IPC/2006/11. New and Geneva.

UNCTAD (2007b). *Model Law on Competition: Substantive Possible Elements for a competition Law, Commentaries and Alternative Approaches in Existing Legislations.*

UNCTAD (2007c). Report on the UNCTAD meeting on Globalization of Port Logistics: Opportunities and Challenges for Developing Countries. December. Geneva.

UNCTAD (2008a). *Investment Brief Number 2, Aftercare – Reaching out to your Investor Community*. United Nations publication. New York and Geneva.

UNCTAD (2008b). *World Investment Report: Transnational Corporations and the Infrastructure Challenge*. United Nations publication. New York and Geneva.

UNCTAD (2009). *World Investment Report: Transnational Corporations, Agricultural Production and Development*. United Nations publication. New York and Geneva.

UNDP (2005a). *Human Development Report Regional Fact Sheet: Sub-Saharan Africa*. United Nations publication. New York.

UNDP (2005b). *Millennium Development Goals Report for Sierra Leone*. United Nations publication. Freetown.

UNDP (2007). *Sierra Leone Human Development Report: Empowering Local Government for Sustainable Human Development and Poverty Reduction: The District Focus Approach to Development.* United Nations publication. Geneva.

UNESCO (2006). The UNESCO Teacher Training Initiative for sub-Saharan Africa: the Sierra Leone perspective. First Meeting of National Coordinators. Dakar. March.

Unruh JD and Turray H (2006). Land tenure, food security and investment in post-war Sierra Leone. Livelihood Support Programme working paper 22. Food and Agriculture Organization of the United Nations.

Vimetco (2008). Press release: acquisition of bauxite mine in Sierra Leone. July 25. http://www.vimetco.com/news-detail.en/items/acquisition-of-bauxite-mine-in-sierra-leone.html

WEMOS (2001). Poverty Reduction Strategy Papers: What is at stake for health? Papers for the WEMOS meeting on PRSPs.

Woody U (2008). Presentation for the preparation of the Second Poverty Reduction Strategy Paper. Ministry of Trade and Tourism.

World Bank (2000). Gender and growth: Africa's missed potential. *Human Development Macroeconomics.* 197.

World Bank (2005). *Sierra Leone: Tapping the Mineral Wealth for Human Progress - A Break with the Past.* Washington DC, World Bank.

World Bank (2006). *The Sierra Leone Energy Sector: Prospects and Challenges.* Freetown.

World Bank (2007a). *Education in Sierra Leone: Present Challenges, Future Opportunities.* Washington DC.

World Bank (2007b). *Sierra Leone Emergency Power – Meeting the Challenge of Turning on the Lights.* Washington DC.

World Bank (2008). *World Development Indicators.* Washington DC.

World Bank (2009). *Doing Business, Sierra Leone.*

World Diamond Council (2008). The Kimberly Process. http://www.diamondfacts.org

WRI (2003). *Earth Trends: Country Profiles.* Washington DC.

WTO (1995a). Schedule of Specific Commitments. WTO document GATS/SC/105. 30 August.

WTO (1995b). General Agreement on Trade in Services – Sierra Leone's Schedule of Specific Commitments. WTO document GATS/EL/105. 30 August.

WTO (2004). WTO Trade Policy Review of Sierra Leone. WTO document WT/TPR/S/143.

WTO (2007). IP/C/W/499. 3 October.

# SELECTED UNCTAD PUBLICATIONS ON TRANSNATIONAL CORPORATIONS AND FDI

## A. Serial publications

### World Investment Reports

http://www.unctad.org/wir

UNCTAD, World Investment Report 2009. Transnational Corporations, Agricultural Production and Development (New York and Geneva, 2009). 280 pages. Sales No. E.09.II.D.15.

UNCTAD, World Investment Report 2008. Transnational Corporations and the Infrastructure Challenge (New York and Geneva, 2008). 294 pages. Sales No. E.08.II.D.23.

UNCTAD, World Investment Report 2007. Transnational Corporations, Extractive Industries and Development (New York and Geneva, 2007). 294 pages. Sales No. E.07.II.D.9.

UNCTAD, World Investment Report 2006. FDI from Developing and Transition Economies: Implications for Development (New York and Geneva, 2006). 340 pages. Sales No. E.06.II.D.11.

UNCTAD, World Investment Report 2005. Transnational Corporations and the Internationalization of R&D (New York and Geneva, 2005). 332 pages. Sales No. E.05.II.D.10.

UNCTAD, World Investment Report 2004. The Shift Towards Services (New York and Geneva, 2004). 468 pages. Sales No. E.04.II.D.36.

UNCTAD, World Investment Report 2003. FDI Policies for Development: National and International Perspectives (New York and Geneva, 2003). 303 pages. Sales No. E.03.II.D.8.

UNCTAD, World Investment Report 2002: Transnational Corporations and Export Competitiveness (New York and Geneva, 2002). 350 pages. Sales No. E.02.II.D.4.

UNCTAD, World Investment Report 2001: Promoting Linkages (New York and Geneva, 2001). 354 pages. Sales No. E.01.II.D.12.

UNCTAD, World Investment Report 2000: Cross-border Mergers and Acquisitions and Development (New York and Geneva, 2000). 337 pages. Sales No. E.00.II.D.20.

### Investment Policy Reviews

http://www.unctad.org/ipr

UNCTAD, Examen de la Politique d'investissement du Burundi (Geneva, 2010). 118 pages. UNCTAD/DIAE/PCB/2009/17.

UNCTAD, Investment Policy Review of Belarus (Geneva, 2009). 111 pages. UNCTAD/DIAE/PCB/2009/10.

UNCTAD, Examen de la Politique de d'investissement du Burkina Faso (Geneva, 2009). 120 pages. UNCTAD/DIAE/PCB/2009/4.

UNCTAD, Examen de la Politique d'investissement de la Mauritanie (Geneva, 2008). 120 pages. UNCTAD/ITE/IPC/2008/5.

UNCTAD, Investment Policy Review of the Nigeria (Geneva, 2009). 140 pages. UNCTAD/DIAE/PCB/2008/1.

UNCTAD, Investment Policy Review of the Dominican Republic (Geneva, 2008). 116 pages. UNCTAD/ITE/IPC/2007/9.

UNCTAD, Investment Policy Review of Viet Nam (Geneva, 2008). 158 pages. UNCTAD/ITE/IPC/2007/10.

UNCTAD, Examen de la Politique d'investissement du Maroc (Geneva, 2008). 142 pages. UNCTAD/ITE/IPC/2006/16.

UNCTAD, Report on the Implementation of the Investment Policy Review of Uganda (Geneva, 2007) 30 pages. UNCTAD/ITE/IPC/2006/15.

UNCTAD, Investment Policy Review of Zambia (Geneva, 2006). 76 pages. UNCTAD/ITE/IPC/2006/14.

UNCTAD, Investment Policy Review of Rwanda (Geneva, 2006). 136 pages. UNCTAD/ITE/IPC/2006/11.

UNCTAD, Investment Policy Review of Colombia (Geneva, 2006). 86 pages. UNCTAD/ITE/IPC/2005/11.

UNCTAD, Report on the Implementation of the Investment Policy Review of Egypt (Geneva, 2005). 18 pages. UNCTAD/ITE/IPC/2005/7.

UNCTAD, Investment Policy Review of Kenya (Geneva, 2005). 114 pages. UNCTAD/ITE/IPC/2005/8.

UNCTAD, Examen de la Politique d'investissement du Bénin (Geneva, 2005). 126 pages. UNCTAD/ITE/IPC/2004/4.

UNCTAD, Examen de la Politique d'investissement de l'Algérie (Geneva, 2004). 110 pages. UNCTAD/ITE/IPC/2003/9.

UNCTAD, Investment Policy Review of Sri Lanka (Geneva, 2003). 89 pages. UNCTAD/ITE/IPC/2003/8.

UNCTAD, Investment Policy Review of Lesotho (Geneva, 2003). 105 pages. Sales No. E.03.II.D.18.

UNCTAD, Investment Policy Review of Nepal. (Geneva, 2003). 89 pages. Sales No.E.03.II.D.17.

UNCTAD, Investment Policy Review of Ghana (Geneva, 2002). 103 pages. Sales No. E.02.II.D.20.

UNCTAD, Investment Policy Review of Botswana (Geneva, 2003). 107 pages. Sales No. E.03.II.D.1.

UNCTAD, Investment Policy Review of Tanzania (Geneva, 2002). 109 pages. Sales No. E.02.II.D.6. $ 20.

UNCTAD, Investment and Innovation Policy Review of Ethiopia (Geneva, 2001). 130 pages. Sales No. E.01.II.D.5.

UNCTAD, Investment Policy Review of Ecuador. (Geneva, 2001). 136 pages. Sales No. E.01.II.D.31. Also available in Spanish.

UNCTAD, Investment Policy Review of Mauritius (Geneva, 2000). 92 pages. Sales No. E.00.II.D.11.

UNCTAD, Investment Policy Review of Peru (Geneva, 2000). 109 pages. Sales No. E.00.II.D.7.

UNCTAD, Investment Policy Review of Uganda (Geneva, 1999). 71 pages. Sales No. E.99.II.D.24.

UNCTAD, Investment Policy Review of Uzbekistan (Geneva, 1999). 65 pages. Document number: UNCTAD/ITE/IIP/Misc.13.

UNCTAD, Investment Policy Review of Egypt (Geneva, 1999). 119 pages. Sales No. E.99.II.D.20.

## Blue Books on Best Practice in Investment Promotion and Faciliation

UNCTAD, Blue Book on Best Practice in Investment Promotion and Facilitation: Nigeria (Geneva, 2009).

UNCTAD, Blue Book on Best Practice in Investment Promotion and Facilitation: Zambia (Geneva, 2007).

UNCTAD, Blue Book on Best Practice in Investment Promotion and Facilitation: Kenya (Geneva, 2005).

UNCTAD, Blue Book on Best Practice in Investment Promotion and Facilitation: United Republic of Tanzania (Geneva, 2005).

UNCTAD, Blue Book on Best Practice in Investment Promotion and Facilitation: Uganda (Geneva, 2005).

UNCTAD, Blue Book on Best Practice in Investment Promotion and Facilitation: Cambodia (Geneva, 2004).

UNCTAD, Blue Book on Best Practice in Investment Promotion and Facilitation: Lao People's Democratic Republic (Geneva, 2004).

## Investment Guides

http://www.unctad.org/investmentguides

UNCTAD, An Investment Guide to Rwanda: Opportunities and Conditions (Geneva, 2006). Document symbol: UNCTAD/ITE/IIA/2006/3. Free of charge.

UNCTAD, An Investment Guide to Mali: Opportunities and Conditions (Geneva, 2006). Document symbol: UNCTAD/ITE/IIA/2006/2. Free of charge.

UNCTAD and ICC, An Investment Guide to East Africa (Geneva, 2005). Document symbol: UNCTAD/IIA/2005/4. Free of charge.

UNCTAD and ICC, An Investment Guide to Tanzania (Geneva, 2005). Document symbol: UNCTAD/IIA/2005/3. Free of charge.

UNCTAD and ICC, An Investment Guide to Kenya (Geneva, 2005). Document symbol: UNCTAD/IIA/2005/2. Free of charge.

UNCTAD and ICC, An Investment Guide to Mauritania (Geneva, 2004). Document symbol: UNCTAD/IIA/2004/4. Free of charge.

UNCTAD and ICC, An Investment Guide to Cambodia (Geneva, 2003). 89 pages. Document symbol: UNCTAD/IIA/2003/6. Free of charge.

UNCTAD and ICC, An Investment Guide to Nepal (Geneva, 2003). 97 pages. Document symbol: UNCTAD/IIA/2003/2. Free of charge.

UNCTAD and ICC, An Investment Guide to Mozambique (Geneva, 2002). 109 pages. Document symbol: UNCTAD/IIA/4. Free of charge.

UNCTAD and ICC, An Investment Guide to Uganda (Geneva, 2001). 76 pages. Document symbol: UNCTAD/ITE/IIT/Misc.30. Publication updated in 2004. New document symbol UNCTAD/ITE/IIA/2004/3. Free of charge.

UNCTAD and ICC, An Investment Guide to Mali (Geneva, 2001). 105 pages. Document symbol: UNCTAD/ITE/IIT/Misc.24. Publication updated in 2004. New document symbol UNCTAD/ITE/IIA/2004/1. Free of charge.

UNCTAD and ICC, An Investment Guide to Ethiopia (Geneva, 2000). 68 pages. Document symbol: UNCTAD/ITE/IIT/Misc.19. Publication updated in 2004. New document symbol UNCTAD/ITE/IIA/2004/2. Free of charge.

UNCTAD and ICC, An Investment Guide to Bangladesh (Geneva, 2000). 66 pages. Document symbol: UNCTAD/ITE/IIT/Misc.29. Free of charge.

## Issues in International Investment Agreements

http://www.unctad.org/iia

UNCTAD, Bilateral Investment Treaties 1995-2006: Trends in Investment Rulemaking (New York and Geneva, 2006).

UNCTAD, Investment Provisions in Economic Integration Agreements (New York and Geneva, 2006).

UNCTAD, Glossary of Key Concepts Used in IIAs. UNCTAD Series on Issues in International Investment Agreements (New York and Geneva, 2003).

UNCTAD, Incentives UNCTAD Series on Issues in International Investment Agreements (New York and Geneva, 2003). Sales No. E.04.II.D.6. $15.

UNCTAD, Transparency. UNCTAD Series on Issues in International Investment Agreements (New York and Geneva, 2003). Sales No. E.03.II.D.7. $15.

UNCTAD, Dispute Settlement: Investor-State. UNCTAD Series on Issues in International Investment Agreements (New York and Geneva, 2003). 128 pages. Sales No. E.03.II.D.5. $15.

UNCTAD, Dispute Settlement: State-State. UNCTAD Series on Issues in International Investment Agreements (New York and Geneva, 2003). 109 pages. Sales No. E.03.II.D.6 $16.

UNCTAD, Transfer of Technology. UNCTAD Series on Issues on International Investment Agreements (New York and Geneva, 2001). 135 pages. Sales No. E.01.II.D.33. $16.

UNCTAD, Illicit Payments. UNCTAD Series on Issues on International Investment Agreements (New York and Geneva, 2001). 112 pages. Sales No. E.01.II.D.20. $13.

UNCTAD, Home Country Measures. UNCTAD Series on Issues on International Investment Agreements (New York and Geneva, 2001). 95 pages. Sales No. E.01.II.D.19. $12.

UNCTAD, Host Country Operational Measures. UNCTAD Series on Issues on International Investment Agreements (New York and Geneva, 2001). 105 pages. Sales No. E.01.II.D.18. $18.

UNCTAD, Social Responsibility. UNCTAD Series on Issues on International Investment Agreements (New York and Geneva, 2001). 87 pages. Sales No. E.01.II.D.4.$15.

UNCTAD, Environment. UNCTAD Series on Issues on International Investment Agreements (New York and Geneva 2001). 106 pages. Sales No. E.01.II.D.3. $15.

UNCTAD, Transfer of Funds. UNCTAD Series on Issues on International Investment Agreements (New York and Geneva 2000). 79 pages. Sales No. E.00.II.D.38. $10.

UNCTAD, Flexibility for Development. UNCTAD Series on Issues on International Investment Agreements (New York and Geneva 2000). 185 pages. Sales No. E.00.II.D.6. $15.

UNCTAD, Employment. UNCTAD Series on Issues on International Investment Agreements (New York and Geneva, 2000). 64 pages. Sales No. E.00.II.D.15. $12.

UNCTAD, Taxation. UNCTAD Series on Issues on International Investment Agreements (New York and Geneva, 2000). 111 pages. Sales No. E.00.II.D.5. $15.

UNCTAD, Taking of Property. UNCTAD Series on Issues on International Investment Agreements (New York and Geneva, 2000). 78 pages. Sales No. E.00.II.D.4. $12.

## International Investment Instruments

UNCTAD's Work Programme on International Investment Agreements: From UNCTAD IX to UNCTAD X. Document symbol: UNCTAD/ITE/IIT/Misc.26. Available free of charge.

UNCTAD, Progress Report. Work undertaken within UNCTAD's work programme on International Investment Agreements between the 10th Conference of UNCTAD 10th Conference of UNCTAD, Bangkok, February 2000, and July 2002 (New York and Geneva, 2002). UNCTAD/ITE/Misc.58. Available free of charge.

UNCTAD, Bilateral Investment Treaties in the Mid-1990s (New York and Geneva, 1998). 322 pages. Sales No. E.98.II.D.8. $46.

UNCTAD, Bilateral Investment Treaties: 1959-1999 (Geneva and New York, 2000) Sales No. E.92.II.A.16. $22.

UNCTAD, International Investment Instruments: A Compendium (New York and Geneva, 1996 to 2003). 12 volumes. Vol. I: Sales No. E.96.A.II.A.9. Vol. II: Sales No. E.96.II.A.10. Vol. III: Sales No. E.96.II.A.11. Vol. IV: Sales No. E.00.II.D.13. Vol. V: Sales No. E.00.II.A.14. Vol. VI: Sales No. E.01.II.D.34. Vol. VII: Sales No. E.02.II.D.14. Vol. VIII: Sales No. E.02.II.D.15. Vol. IX: Sales No. E.02.II.D.16. Vol. X: Sales No. E.02.II.D.21. Vol. XI: Sales No. E.04.II.D.9. Vol. XII: Sales No. E.04.II.D.10. $60.

## ASIT Advisory Studies

http://www.unctad.org/asit

Investment Advisory Series, Series A, Number 1 (2007). Aftercare. A core function in investment promotion. Geneva.

No. 17. The World of Investment Promotion at a Glance: A Survey of Investment Promotion Practices. UNCTAD/ITE/IPC/3. Free of charge.

No. 16. Tax Incentives and Foreign Direct Investment: A Global Survey. 180 p. Sales No. E.01.II.D.5.

No. 15. Investment Regimes in the Arab World: Issues and Policies. 232 p. Sales No. E/F.00.II.D.32.

No. 14. Handbook on Outward Investment Promotion Agencies and Institutions. 50 p. Sales No. E.99.II.D.22.

No. 13. Survey of Best Practices in Investment Promotion. 71 p. Sales No. E.97.II.D.11.

## B. Individual Studies

UNCTAD, Investment and Technology Policies for Competitiveness: Review of Successful Country Experiences (Geneva, 2003). Document symbol: UNCTAD/ITE/ICP/2003/2.

UNCTAD, The Development Dimension of FDI: Policy and Rule-Making Perspectives (Geneva, 2003). Sales No. E.03.II.D.22. $35.

UNCTAD, FDI and Performance Requirements: New Evidence from Selected Countries (Geneva, 2003). Sales No. E.03.II.D.32. 318 pages. $ 35.

UNCTAD, Measures of the Transnationalization of Economic Activity (New York and Geneva, 2001). Document symbol: UNCTAD/ITE/IIA/1. Sales No. E.01.II.D.2.

UNCTAD, FDI Determinants and TNC Strategies: The Case of Brazil (Geneva, 2000). Sales No. E.00:II.D.2.

UNCTAD, The Competitiveness Challenge: Transnational Corporations and Industrial Restructuring in Developing Countries (Geneva, 2000). Sales No. E.00.II.D.35.

UNCTAD, Foreign Direct Investment in Africa: Performance and Potential (Geneva, 1999). Document symbol: UNCTAD/ITE/IIT/Misc.15. Available free of charge.

UNCTAD, The Financial Crisis in Asia and Foreign Direct Investment An Assessment (Geneva, 1998). 110 pages. Sales No. GV.E.98.0.29. $20.

UNCTAD, Handbook on Foreign Direct Investment by Small and Medium-sized Enterprises: Lessons from Asia (New York and Geneva, 1998). 202 pages. Sales No. E.98.II.D.4. $48.

UNCTAD, Handbook on Foreign Direct Investment by Small and Medium-sized Enterprises: Lessons from Asia. Executive Summary and Report on the Kunming Conference. 70 pages. Document symbol: UNCTAD/ITE/IIT/6 (Summary). Available free of charge.

UNCTAD, Incentives and Foreign Direct Investment (New York and Geneva, 1996). Current Studies, Series A, No. 30. 98 pages. Sales No. E.96.II.A.6. $25.

UNCTC, Foreign Direct Investment in the People's Republic of China (New York, 1988). 110 pages. Sales No. E.88.II.A.3. Out of print. Available on microfiche. Paper copy from microfiche: $122.

UNCTAD, Foreign Direct Investment, Trade, Aid and Migration Current Studies, Series A, No. 29. (A joint publication with the International Organization for Migration, Geneva, 1996). 90 pages. Sales No. E.96M.A.8. $25.

UNCTAD, Explaining and Forecasting Regional Flows of Foreign Direct Investment (New York, 1993). Current Studies, Series A, No. 26. 58 pages. Sales No. E.94.II.A.5. $25.

UNCTAD, Small and Medium-sized Transnational Corporations: Role, Impact and Policy Implications (New York and Geneva, 1993). 242 pages. Sales No. E.93.II.A. 15. $35.

UNCTAD, Small and Medium-sized Transnational Corporations: Executive Summary and Report of the Osaka Conference (Geneva, 1994). 60 pages. Available free of charge.

## C. Journals

Transnational Corporations Journal (formerly The CTC Reporter). Published three times a year. Annual subscription price: $45; individual issues $20.

# READERSHIP SURVEY

## Investment Policy Review of Sierra Leone

In order to improve the quality and relevance of the work of UNCTAD's Division on Investment and Enterprise, it would be useful to receive the views of readers on this publication. It would therefore be greatly appreciated if you could complete the following questionnaire and return it to:

Readership Survey
UNCTAD Division on Investment and Enterprise
United Nations Office in Geneva
Palais des Nations, Room E-9123
CH-1211 Geneva 10, Switzerland
Fax: 41-22-917-0197

1. Name and address of respondent (optional):

_____
_____

2. Which of the following best describes your area of work?

Government ○　　Public enterprise ○
Private enterprise ○　　Academic or research ○
International organization ○　　Media ○
Not-for-profit organization ○　　Other (specify) _____

3. In which country do you work? _____

4. What is your assessment of the contents of this publication?

Excellent ○　　Adequate ○
Good ○　　Poor ○

5. How useful is this publication to your work?

Very useful ○　　Somewhat useful ○　　Irrelevant ○

6. Please indicate the three things you liked best about this publication and are useful to your work:

_____
_____
_____

7. Please indicate the three things you liked least about this publication:

_____
_____

8.      If you have read other publications of the UNCTAD Division on Investment and Enterprise, what is your overall assessment of them?

Consistently good  ◯        Usually good, but with some exceptions  ◯
Generally mediocre  ◯        Poor                                     ◯

9.    On the average, how useful are those publications to you in your work?

Very useful        ◯        Somewhat useful  ◯        Irrelevant  ◯

10.    Are you a regular recipient of Transnational Corporations (formerly The CTC Reporter), UNCTAD-DIAE's tri-annual refereed journal?

Yes              ◯        No              ◯

If not, please check here if you would like to receive a sample copy sent to the name and address you have given above    ◯

# UNITED NATIONS PUBLICATIONS
# MAY BE OBTAINED FROM
# BOOKSTORES AND DISTRIBUTORS
# THROUGHOUT THE WORLD.
# PLEASE CONSULT YOUR BOOKSTORE OR WRITE TO:

**For Africa and Europe to:**

Sales Section
United Nations Office at Geneva
Palais des Nations
CH-1211 Geneva 10
Switzerland
Tel: (41-22) 917-1234
Fax: (41-22) 917-0123
E-mail: unpubli@unog.ch

**For Asia and the Pacific, the Caribbean, Latin America and North America to:**

Sales Section
Room DC2-0853
United Nations Secretariat
New York, NY 10017
United States
Tel: (1-212) 963-8302 or (800) 253-9646
Fax: (1-212) 963-3489
E-mail: publications@un.org

All prices are quoted in United States dollars.

**For further information on the work of the
Division on Investment and Enterprise, UNCTAD,
please address inquiries to:**

United Nations Conference on Trade and Development
Division on Investment and Enterprise
Palais des Nations, Room E-10054
CH-1211 Geneva 10, Switzerland
Telephone: (41-22) 917-5534
Fax: (41-22) 917-0498
http://www.unctad.org